RADIANT

MAFALDA
PINTO LEITE

RADIANT
THE COOKBOOK

Roost Books
Boulder
2018

Roost Books
An imprint of Shambhala Publications, Inc.
4720 Walnut Street
Boulder, Colorado 80301
roostbooks.com

9 8 7 6 5 4 3 2 1

First Edition
Printed in China

⊗ This edition is printed on acid-free
paper that meets the American National
Standards Institute Z39.48 Standard.
♲ Shambhala Publications makes every
effort to print on recycled paper. For more
information please visit www.shambhala.com.

Roost Books is distributed worldwide
by Penguin Random House Inc., and its
subsidiaries.

Cover and book design by
Shubhani Sarkar, sarkardesignstudio.com

Library of Congress
Cataloging-in-Publication Data

Names: Pinto Leite, Mafalda, author.
Title: Radiant: the cookbook /
    Mafalda Pinto Leite.
Description: First edition. | Boulder:
    Roost Books, 2018. | Includes index.
Identifiers: LCCN 2017040167 | ISBN
    9781611805093 (hardcover: alk. paper)
Subjects: LCSH: Cooking. | Beauty,
    Personal. | Functional foods. | LCGFT:
    Cookbooks.
Classification: LCC TX714 .L444 2018 |
    DDC 641.5—dc23
LC record available at https://lccn.loc.
    gov/2017040167

TO MY CHILDREN, MARINA, VASCO, GRAÇA, AND DIOGO
FOR MOLDING ME INTO THE BEST VERSION OF MYSELF.

CONTENTS

INTRODUCTION

Food is our most powerful ally for aging gracefully. We all want to look and feel our very best, but in our quest to do so, we can sometimes fall prey to beauty experts inviting us to try the newest antiaging miracle cures. This book is my antidote to those beauty myths—it is informed and inspired by my own personal journey as a woman, chef, health coach, and mother.

I learned a lot about the power of foods and botanicals early on in cooking school, where the motto was "For Food and Health" and the focus was on how magical and powerful certain ingredients can be. I also studied Ayurveda in depth and learned about how plants can affect our wellness, beauty, and overall longevity. The good news is that we don't need to look to a miracle product to make us feel radiant and confident. The solution has been hiding in plain sight all along. You have everything you need to be beautiful right here, right now: all you need is a well-stocked pantry and a refrigerator full of nutrient-rich foods. Beauty is about nourishing your body from the inside out, not about putting creams or serums on your face. Our skin can survive without any miracle collagen serum, but it absolutely cannot thrive without healthy fats, protein, and essential nutrients. The same goes for our hair, nails, eyes, teeth, and bones. You can get all the healthy fats, proteins, and nutrients your body needs from plant-based foods, and in fact they are the most amazing beauty fuel, giving your body all the energy it needs to defend, repair, renew, and fortify.

You may be amazed at how the smallest things can make a big impact. One of my favorite examples is just a pinch of schisandra berry powder in your morning drink; in a matter of a few days, your face will feel velvety smooth and incredibly firm. And, just by eating more greens every day, your skin will glow all the time. That is the power of food.

Radiant is not about rigid rules, crazy detoxes, and obsessing about the foods you can't eat. My hope is that this book will guide you to all the amazing foods *you can and should have* in abundance, and show you how amazing you feel when you eat them on a regular basis. And if you do have a favorite treat, I'm a big believer in finding a healthy alternative that tastes equally delicious, as you'll see in the dessert chapter. *Radiant* is not about missing out—it's about falling in love with real foods and the joy of feeling and seeing the difference those foods make to your skin and your overall well-being.

THE INSIDE OUT APPROACH

The skin is a living organ (the largest one you have), and it's the only organ that is fully exposed to the environment. Unlike our lungs or heart, our skin is continuously subject to destructive effects from the outside world. Our skin, hair, and nails get bombarded every day by ultraviolet rays,

BEAUTY BENEFITS 101

Here is a quick and easy guide to terms I use to examine the amazing array of beautifying foods and describe their powerful effects on our skin and overall health.

COLLAGEN

Collagen promotes skin elasticity, preventing the onset of lines and wrinkles. Foods with collagen help skin look firmer and support skin cells in renewing and repairing normally.

HYDRATING

Staying hydrated is one of the most important ways to be radiant from the inside out. Foods with a high water content help the skin maintain its moisture for a smoother, healthier, and more radiant complexion.

ANTIOXIDANTS

These powerful substances repair and rejuvenate skin cells by protecting them from free-radical damage.

ANTIAGING

Certain foods can slow down the aging process and promote longevity due to their complexion-boosting nutrients.

ANTI-INFLAMMATORY

By decreasing inflammation in joints, tissues, and organs, certain foods contribute to overall balance and longevity, helping to prevent premature aging as well as fighting against chronic diseases.

IMMUNE SYSTEM BOOSTING

Foods can support your immune system by stimulating and supplementing your body's inherent disease- and infection-fighting properties, helping you to live both healthier and longer.

SKIN FOOD

These foods repair and rejuvenate the cells, promoting glowing skin and stimulating cellular restoration, preservation, and longevity.

STRESS REDUCING

Some plant foods contain substances that soothe the nervous system and help restore your body and mind to its natural state of well-being.

METABOLISM BOOSTING

Metabolism is the process of your body converting food into energy. Eating the right foods will jump-start your metabolism, helping with weight management and giving you more energy.

environmental pollution in the air, chemicals in our water—not to mention the things we intentionally do to ourselves, like blow-drying, brushing, covering in make-up, and so on. For all these reasons, our skin demands special attention. We can't do much to influence the weather and outside forces, but we can reclaim our health and beauty by choosing foods that work overtime on our behalf. And that is what the inside out approach is all about—I hope to empower you to make the right decisions and inspire you to choose a life of vibrancy and radiant health.

Food is where it all begins. When you fill yourself up with the most alive, vibrant foods on the planet, you are not only nourishing your body, but your skin, your mind, and your entire immune system. From foods that target tissue regrowth and promote gut health to mineral-dense foods that feed the skin and calm the nervous system—these powerful beauty allies are here to help us. Not only will these foods feed your skin, but they can be life changing—feeding your creativity, joy, and overall happiness.

The key is to make sure we eat a variety of quality plant-based foods. Eating a rainbow of plant foods ensures you're getting the full spectrum of nutrients your body needs in order to function at an optimal level. Did you know that beets not only help hydrate dry skin and improve your complexion, but they also help reduce inflammation throughout the body? Or that avocados are super high in vitamin E, one of the most powerful antioxidants, and are also a natural wrinkle reducer? How about that vitamin C, found in so many of our favorite fruits, not only boosts your immune system but also fights against acne and scars *and* brightens and evens out your overall complexion? Even the common carrot is a powerhouse for your skin, with its large amounts of beta-carotene, a powerful antioxidant that combats free radicals—the waste products from the body's conversion of food into energy—which break down collagen (your skin's support structure). Beta-carotene also lessens the skin's sensitivity to the sun, providing some natural protection against sun-induced redness and pigmentation.

The foods we choose to eat can help us receive life-force energy—clearing our mind, our body, and our skin—and bring us back to our natural, balanced state of well-being. This way of eating is not about labels and restrictions—you don't have to be vegan or gluten free—but the more live, plant-based foods you eat, the more energy you will have. You don't have to be a raw foodist, either, nor should you feel bad about eating cooked foods. A whole-food, plant-based diet is all about making the most out of high-quality ingredients that have a myriad of health benefits. Plants, fruits, and vegetables are the most beautifying foods because of how nutrient dense and hydrating they are, which is paramount when it comes to balanced nutrition and beauty. This way of eating doesn't require following strict rules, but rather uses food as medicine to help balance, restore, and heal your body so you can look and feel your absolute best.

It can be overwhelming to change the way you think about food, but having a well-stocked pantry is the best way to manifest your dream of radiant health. You should start by donating or recycling all the beauty aggressor ingredients you currently have (for example, white sugar, white flour, and so on). Try making a list of the most nourishing, beautifying ingredients, and stock your kitchen with these wonderful foods so you won't be tempted to eat anything that doesn't benefit you or your glow. When you go to the store, be guided by what's in season. Get excited by what's on hand this day, in this season; let your body guide you to what it wants to be filled with. Look for colors, textures, smells. Quit counting your calories and count beauty nutrients instead! How much color can you feed your body with in one day? And remember to go back to basics: as long as it grows from the ground and is organic, you're in loving hands.

Every item in your pantry should be filled to the brim with beauty benefits—ingredients make all the difference. When I have all my best ingredients on hand, I feel more balanced, energized, happy, and healthy, and this affects everything: my family life, my work, and my feeling of well-being.

In the following pages you'll find all the nutrient-rich foods you need so you can eat this way every day. As you read, try to remain open to exploring these ideas and recipes, then just use what resonates with you and what makes sense for your daily needs. The transformation begins when you take your innate beauty and well-being into your own hands.

PART ONE

THE RADIANT KITCHEN

BASICS FOR A RADIANT YOU

It can be a challenge to take care of ourselves every day. Happily, there are a few simple steps that you can add to your daily routine to enhance your overall beauty and happiness. As you take a little time to rethink and restart your diet, try to keep these fourteen basics in mind—think of them as the outline for your own personal beauty boot camp! Listed in no particular order, all these elements work together holistically and synergistically for a more beautiful you.

EAT MORE RAW FOODS.

Eat more fresh, raw food—but start slow, especially if you're new to it. Take small steps by adding a green juice every day. After a couple weeks, begin eating an entire raw meal on a couple of days in a row. You don't have to become a raw foodist to feel the power of living foods—preparing raw food can be as basic as peeling a banana. There are so many benefits to be reaped: bountiful energy, acute brain power, luminous skin, elevated mood, and restored digestion and assimilation.

GO ORGANIC.

My weekly farmer's market visit is an essential part of my routine—I just love to get inspiration for making meals from organic, local, seasonal ingredients. I believe we are meant to eat foods in their natural state, as close to where they were originally grown as possible. Organically grown food has no harmful chemicals, pesticides, waxes, or residues, and the added benefit of more nutrition. By eating these foods we are also sending a clear message of health to the body, down to a cellular level. So if you want to achieve gorgeous, glowing skin, one of the first steps is to decrease your toxic load by choosing organic, chemical-free fruits and vegetables and by avoiding additives and preservatives in foods.

CUT THE SUGAR.

Consuming refined sugars can result in damaged proteins, including those powerhouses for the skin, collagen and elastin. These are the key protein fibers that keep your skin firm and elastic. Refined sugars create imbalance and inflammation and also lead to depleted energy. Luckily, there are many healthy alternatives that will satisfy any sweet tooth (see page 54 on sweeteners). Eating a low-glycemic diet is also crucial for the proper functioning of your endocrine system, vital organs, and gut health. After you kick the refined sugar habit you will feel more energetic and have more radiant skin.

LOAD UP ON ENZYMES.

Enzymes are essential for all of the biochemical reactions that happen
in your body—from digestion, energy production, nutrient absorption,
detoxification, and hormone production to taming inflammation and
slowing the aging process. Enzymes can even help to repair our DNA and
RNA, increasing our vitality and improving the turnover and repair of our
skin cells.

Digestive enzymes break down your food so that it may be better
assimilated into every cell in your body. They also help to heal your gut and
elevate your mood, and they boost your metabolism, brain function, energy,
and immune support. When you cook food, many of the naturally occurring
enzymes are destroyed due to high temperatures and water loss, so to load up
on enzymes, eat more raw foods.

Powerfully enzyme-rich foods include soaked and sprouted nuts and
seeds, pineapple, papaya, mango, avocado, raw honey and bee pollen, extra-
virgin olive oil, and coconut oil.

EAT AN ALKALINE DIET.

Creating a proper balance of acidity to alkalinity within the body (that is,
a pH of 7.3 to 7.4) is crucial for good health and vitality. This is not to say
that you should only eat alkaline foods, but striving for a proper balance
helps promote radiant, healthy skin and clear, bright eyes. Acid-forming
foods aren't bad in and of themselves—the problem is that most people
consume too much of them, which creates an environment where disease and
inflammation can thrive. To keep your constitution more alkaline, you will
want to have a good amount of green leafy vegetables or sea vegetables like
kale and hijiki. Drinking a simple green juice is also a great way to balance
your system when you need to reset.

EAT GOOD FATS.

Good fats are key to graceful aging and a healthy complexion. Eating the
right kind of fats ensures that we have the essential fatty acids (EFAs) that
our bodies are incapable of producing on their own. These fatty acids are
great for protecting our skin, but they are also essential for brain function,
hormone production, metabolism, weight loss, energy, and immune function.

Your brain is 60 percent fat, and the fat you eat literally feeds your brain,
boosting cognition, happiness, learning, and memory. Healthy cell walls
made from high-quality fats are better able to metabolize insulin, which keeps
blood sugar regulated. It's also important to familiarize yourself with which
fats are the best to cook with and which are better consumed unheated. When
a fat reaches its smoke point, its structure changes and it becomes rancid,
releasing free radicals that stress and damage on a cellular level throughout
the body. Raw plant fats like avocado, coconut, nuts, seeds, and extra-virgin

olive oil can enhance your energy, stabilize your hormones, nourish your nervous system, beautify and cleanse your skin, and boost your overall immunity.

DISCOVER ADAPTOGENS.

Adaptogenic herbs have been used in traditional Chinese and Ayurvedic medicine for centuries. These herbs help our bodies cope with stress and change. They are named for their unique ability to "adapt" their function according to the body's specific needs. This unique group of herbs can improve the health of your adrenal system, which is in charge of managing your body's hormonal response to stress and anxiety. They allow our bodies to absorb nutrients so that we have optimal energy and increased metabolism, immunity, and libido and, at the same time, less inflammation, stress, and fatigue. You must be patient—their effects may initially be subtle, and they tend to act slowly—but the benefits will be undeniable and long lasting.

These rejuvenating herbs can be easily blended into hot or cold liquids to be enjoyed during the day as a major pick-me-up. Some examples of adaptogens are reishi, which boosts metabolism and alleviates stress; ashwagandha, which alleviates adrenal fatigue and is anti-inflammatory; schisandra, which is collagen building and aphrodisiac; and cordyceps, an antioxidant that boosts immunity. (See the Drinks chapter, page 67, for smoothies and other drink recipes that incorporate "Beauty Add-Ins" like these herbs.)

FOCUS ON THE BREATH.

Simple as it may sound, in our fast-paced world we often don't realize how shallow our breathing actually is. Become aware of your breath: how deep is it? Shallow breathing creates stagnation in the blood, while deep breathing reduces stress and anxiety. In addition, higher amounts of oxygen in the bloodstream have an alkalizing effect on your body's pH. So start to pay attention to your breath: set aside five minutes a day to sit and focus on deep breathing, and you'll see how you will feel instantaneously relaxed and rejuvenated.

GET YOUR BEAUTY SLEEP.

Sleep is absolutely essential for inner and outer beauty, because it is crucial for overall wellness and vitality. Getting enough sleep at night can control weight gain, help you to manage stress levels, and even prevent wrinkle formation. Aim for a minimum of eight hours of uninterrupted sleep.

MOVE YOUR BODY.

The more you sweat, the more toxins are released. The fewer toxins in your system, the less acidic your body becomes. Exercise regularly, at least thirty minutes daily, to keep the lymph system flowing and to build more alkaline blood. This can be anything you enjoy. Yoga, going for a brisk walk, dancing, and running are some of my favorites. Whatever you choose, be sure to get your heart rate up and get some sweat going, as this gets the detoxifying organs and systems "moving." Exercise also helps to relieve stress and anxiety.

TRY DRY BRUSHING.

One third of toxins are released through our skin, our largest organ. Typically, if there is something not quite right going on in your body, it will show up in some way on your skin, whether it's a rash, a breakout, bloating, or cellulite. By dry brushing your body you are helping to reduce fluid retention and cellulite, stimulate circulation, improve skin tone, boost immunity, and increase lymph flow, working toward radiantly healthy skin. Regular vigorous skin brushing can even help regenerate collagen over time. It should always be done with a dry brush in long, circular strokes. Start with your feet all the way up to your heart and then from your hands all the way up your arms to your heart. Always brush toward your heart.

DRINK MORE WATER.

Need a quick beauty boost? Grab a glass of water. We all know that water is important for our health—but did you know all the amazing things it does for your appearance? Believe it or not, drinking enough water each and every day can be the answer to your biggest beauty problems (think dull skin, brittle nails, and even thinning hair). Adequate H2O doesn't just quench your thirst, it also helps your body flush out toxins more efficiently, leaving your skin looking fresh as a result. Truthfully, a gallon a day won't magically erase fine lines and wrinkles, but by staying hydrated you can maintain your skin's natural elasticity and suppleness. So drink up!

GIVE YOURSELF A MASSAGE.

Taking care of ourselves is so important, but we often tend to put our loved ones first and, at the end of the day, we don't take the time to care for ourselves. Finding some easy self-care rituals to build into your weekly routine can be transformative. A massage is a wonderful way to start—try Abhyanga, an ancient Ayurvedic practice of self-massage that you can do by taking a few extra minutes in the shower. Before you turn the water on, stand in the shower with a cup of warmed coconut oil (or oil of your choice) and spend ten minutes massaging your entire body using circular movements. Start with your feet or arms, wherever is most convenient and comfortable, and move toward your heart. You can finish by scrubbing yourself with a chickpea flour, or almond pulp left over from making almond milk. (Coarse salt and sugar scrubs are not ideal for sensitive skin types, so I usually recommend only the flour or pulp; it's more nourishing and hydrating.) Abhyanga is a practice that sweetly nourishes and soothes the nerves, helps with lymphatic circulation, and makes for the loveliest soft, flushed skin.

MEDITATE.

Meditation is a great way to reduce stress and anxiety by giving yourself the time to breathe and gain perspective. When you meditate, even if only for a few minutes a day, you are allowing your mind and body to enter a more relaxed state. This will release chemicals that counter the chemicals and hormones that are a reaction to stress. Practicing calm, deep breathing also helps oxygenate our bodies, and both the breathing and the state of calm that results help with toxin elimination. Meditation can fundamentally change how your brain and body function—and that can affect how your skin looks. Studies have shown that just eight weeks of regular meditation can actually change the brain's structure by increasing the "cortical thickness" in the part of the brain that helps control good things (like learning and memory) and decreasing it in the parts of the brain responsible for undesirables (like anxiety and stress). This translates into less inflammation in the body, which leads to more lustrous skin and a stronger immune system.

BEAUTY NUTRIENTS

It's never too late to start consuming nutrient-dense, antioxidant-rich, clean, and unadulterated foods that will contribute to your beauty, health, and longevity. Just taking the time to think about the ingredients that go into the foods you are eating and how they affect you from the inside out is very empowering. Begin by rethinking the way you look at the ingredients that make up your meals, and start indulging in nutrient-dense foods that will help you both look and feel better.

VITAMIN A

There are two types of vitamin A. Preformed vitamin A is found in animal products such as meat, fish, poultry, and dairy. Provitamin A is found in plant foods such as fruits and vegetables. The most common type of provitamin A is beta-carotene, which aids in the growth and repair of body tissues and maintenance of healthy hair, nails, teeth, and bones. In skin care, vitamin A also has many names—*retinol* is the most common—with proven benefits like increased cell turnover, which leads to fewer breakouts, better skin tone, a glowing complexion, and a boost in collagen production for firmer skin and fewer wrinkles.
Food sources: Beet greens, blue-green algae (such as spirulina and E3live), cantaloupe, carrots, collards, kale, parsley, romaine lettuce, spinach, sweet potatoes, Swiss chard, winter squash

B VITAMINS

B vitamins provide the energy your skin cells need to regenerate and renew. A good balance keeps skin smooth, hydrated, and glowing.
B1 (thiamine) contributes to strong, lustrous hair.
Food sources: Beet greens, broccoli, green peas, romaine, spinach
B2 (riboflavin) is critical for healthy hair, nails, and skin.
Food sources: Asparagus, beet greens, broccoli, chard, collards, kale, spinach, turnip greens
B3 (niacin or niacin amide) helps to keep skin hydrated.
Food sources: Asparagus, green peas
B5 (pantothenic acid) hydrates, heals, and protects the skin.
Food sources: Avocados, broccoli, shiitake mushrooms, sunflower seeds, sun-dried tomatoes
B6 (pyridoxine) is an antioxidant and is essential for collagen production, which contributes to strong hair and nails.
Food sources: Asparagus, bell peppers, hazelnuts, pistachios, sesame seeds, sunflower seeds
B7 (biotin) contributes to strong, lustrous hair.
Food sources: Avocados, bananas, cauliflower, nuts, sunflower seeds

B9 (folic acid) not only helps to grow strong, lustrous hair, but it repairs DNA and skin cells.
Food sources: Asparagus, avocados, broccoli, lettuce, oranges, spinach
B12 (cobalamin) is also important for strong, lustrous hair.
Food sources: Small amounts are available from mushrooms, some fermented foods like kimchi, kombucha, miso, and sauerkraut, nori, nutritional yeast

VITAMIN C

Vitamin C is a powerful antioxidant found in abundance in many fruits and vegetables. Also known as L-ascorbic acid, it helps the body repair damaged tissue and assists in the production of collagen. As we age, our bodies lose the ability to produce collagen at the same rate as when we were young. Adding that extra vitamin C both internally and topically can help reduce sagging skin, fine lines, and wrinkles. If that weren't enough, studies show that foods high in vitamin C can help protect skin from harmful ultraviolet rays by increasing the effectiveness of sunscreen. Vitamin C also boosts immunity. To get the highest amounts of natural vitamin C, eat raw, locally grown veggies and fruit, as vitamin C levels begin to decline after the produce has been picked and are reduced by cooking. You can also dab your skin with a little fresh lemon juice to help with oily skin, clogged pores, and age spots.
Food sources: Broccoli, cantaloupe, cauliflower, oranges and other citrus fruits, papaya, pineapple, red bell peppers, strawberries

VITAMIN D

Vitamin D acts as a prohormone and effects hormone balance, immune regulation, and mental well-being. It plays a central role in building muscle strength and bone density, repairing skin damage, supporting heart health, and bolstering the entire immune system. A small amount of daily sun exposure can support the natural production of vitamin D in your skin, but many of us are inside all day and have few opportunities to get sufficient sun exposure to prevent vitamin D deficiency (a minimum of 20 minutes per day with at least 20 percent of the body uncovered). Symptoms often manifest as poor energy, insomnia, a compromised immune system, and mood imbalance.
Food sources: Shiitake mushrooms

VITAMIN E

Vitamin E, also called tocopherol, helps tighten and firm the skin. It has antioxidant properties that help fight the damaging and aging effects of free radicals from ultraviolet rays and pollution. Vitamin E stimulates collagen production, protects DNA from damage and the effects of pollution, and hydrates skin from the inside out. Vitamin E is also involved in healthy immune function, gene expression, blood circulation, and good vision. Our bodies cannot make vitamin E, so it's important to get enough through our diet.
Food sources: Almonds, avocados, butternut squash, kale, olives, papaya, parsley, spinach, sunflower seeds, sweet potatoes, Swiss chard

VITAMIN K

There are two types of vitamin K: vitamin K1 and vitamin K2. Vitamin K1 is found in vegetables, and vitamin K2 (also called menaquinone) is found in dairy products and is also produced by the bacteria in your gut. When it comes to skin, vitamin K can help minimize spider veins, bruising, scars, and stretch marks. Getting enough vitamin K2 can help to boost the skin's elasticity which can help prevent wrinkles and lines as well as promote faster healing from within. As we age, the padding beneath our eyes begins to thin, contributing to the look of dark, sunken circles. The best way to treat dark circles caused by aging is to up your vitamin K intake. This amazing vitamin also helps lighten skin discoloration, diminish age spots, and reduce puffiness.
Food sources: Basil, broccoli, Brussels sprouts, cucumbers, ghee, grass-fed butter, green onions, leafy greens such as kale, parsley

ALPHA-LIPOIC ACID (ALA)

Alpha-lipoic acid (ALA) is an antioxidant found in every cell of your body, and it attacks free radicals, which can cause illness and cell degeneration. Specifically, it protects vitamins C and E and boosts their ability to fight free radicals in the body, slowing the aging process. It's also a highly effective anti-inflammatory and protects skin from ultraviolet damage, reducing fine lines.
Food sources: Beets, carrots, broccoli, Brussels sprouts, spinach, tomatoes

CALCIUM

Calcium is by far the most abundant mineral in the body, and 99 percent of it is stored in the bones and teeth. We all know that calcium is critical for strong bones, teeth, nails, and hair, but it also helps the outer layer of the skin regulate cell turnover, replacing old skin cells with new ones, and promotes collagen formation for plumper, smoother skin. So the appearance of your skin can be affected by whether or not enough calcium is available to use during new skin growth and turnover. Ultimately, if your skin does not have enough calcium, the regeneration process slows, and your skin may start to appear thin, fragile, and aged.
Food sources: Almonds, broccoli, chia seeds, dark leafy greens (especially kale), oranges, sea vegetables (especially kelp), sesame seeds

COPPER

The main difference between younger and older blood is the activity caused by a small copper-binding peptide known as GHK. These peptides are short proteins that can help replenish your skin's appearance, keeping it nourished and hydrated and accelerating the healing of topical wounds. Copper can also help revitalize mature skin, improving its elasticity, firmness, and thickness while reducing wrinkles, hyperpigmentation, and sun damage. Copper helps to activate antioxidants that protect against environmental stressors and fight inflammation.

Food sources: Coconut water, dark leafy greens, mushrooms, nuts (especially almonds, cashews, and macadamia nuts), raw cacao, sesame seeds, sunflower seeds, sun-dried tomatoes

COQ10

CoQ10, also known as ubiquinone, is an enzyme that can be found in each and every cell and tissue in our bodies. It is an essential nutrient that helps us produce energy, neutralizes free radicals, and keeps our cells healthy. When we are younger, we can produce as much CoQ10 as we need, but as we age, our levels start to drop. We need CoQ10 to produce collagen and elastin, preventing fine lines and sagging. It is also a strong antioxidant and neutralizes the harmful free radicals that are one of the major causes of aging.

Food sources: Avocados, broccoli, cauliflower, oranges, parsley, pistachios, sesame seeds, spinach, strawberries

GLUTATHIONE

Glutathione is your body's most powerful antioxidant and detoxifying agent. A very simple molecule that is produced naturally in your body, it is found in every cell, with particularly high concentrations in the liver. The amount of glutathione in our cells can be an indicator of how long we have to live. This molecule is essential for eliminating toxins from your body, keeping disease at bay, maintaining youth, and sustaining wellness. As we get older, glutathione levels drop approximately 10 percent every ten years. This can result in an increased susceptibility to metabolic stress, a factor that greatly accelerates the aging process.

Food sources: Asparagus, avocados, broccoli, Brussels sprouts, cabbage, cardamom, cauliflower, cinnamon, garlic, kale, onions, parsley, spinach, turmeric, watercress, watermelon rind

IODINE

Iodine is a micronutrient present in trace amounts in many of the foods we eat. It is present throughout the body in just about every organ and tissue as it is needed by almost every bodily system to keep us alive and energized. For this reason, an iodine deficiency poses many risks, and because the body cannot produce iodine, we have to get it from food. Iodine promotes thyroid health and can help with a whole host of related hormone irregularities. Getting enough iodine in your diet will help to create hydrated skin and healthy, strong hair and boost your metabolism.

Food sources: Avocados, Brazil nuts, coconut oil, ghee, maca root, sea vegetables (especially dulse, kelp, and nori)

IRON

Feeling tired? Do you have puffy eyes? Maybe you have an iron deficiency. Iron is a trace mineral found in every living cell in your body, a primary component of two proteins: hemoglobin (the part of the red blood cell that

11

carries oxygen to the body's tissues) and myoglobin (the part of the muscle cells that hold oxygen). When you have enough iron, your blood cells are strong and carry life-giving oxygen throughout your body. Your metabolism, which relies on oxygen, stays active and you feel stronger and more clear-headed.

Food sources: Dark leafy greens (especially spinach and Swiss chard), nuts, pumpkin seeds, sesame seeds, squash

MAGNESIUM

Magnesium is a critical component of over three hundred biochemical functions in the body—even glutathione (see page 11) requires magnesium for its synthesis. We usually associate it with the muscles, as it can help with cramping and better flexibility, but what is less known is that it is a necessary electrolyte essential for proper hydration. In this way, it can help your skin's overall appearance by reducing acne and other skin disorders for a smooth and glowing complexion. Serotonin, which relaxes the nervous system and elevates mood, is dependent on magnesium, and it also controls stress hormones, which can lead to a better night's sleep. Chronic stress and heavy workouts can deplete our supply of magnesium.

Food sources: Bananas, broccoli, coconut, dark leafy greens (especially spinach and Swiss chard), matcha, nuts (especially almonds and cashews), pumpkin seeds, raw cacao, sea vegetables, sesame seeds

MANGANESE

Manganese, which is stored in the bones, kidneys, and pancreas, is a trace mineral that supports normal health in several ways, including nutrient absorption, production of digestive enzymes, bone development, and immune system defenses.

As a component of the antioxidant enzyme superoxide dismutase, manganese helps combat the damaging effects of free radicals by converting superoxide, a metabolic byproduct, into safer molecules that won't cause cellular damage. As such, it is an excellent addition to your arsenal of antiaging ingredients.

Food sources: Macadamia nuts, oats, raw cacao, seeds (especially pumpkin, sunflower, flax, and sesame)

ESSENTIAL FATTY ACIDS

Essential fatty acids (EFAs), both omega-3 and omega-6 acids, are crucial for brain development, immune-system function, and blood-pressure regulation. Unfortunately, a lot of us are deficient in omega-3s and consume omega-6s in excess, which is a recipe for inflammation and disease. When you have the proper balance of omega-3s and omega-6s, you can also avoid oily skin. Although it has long been assumed that oils and fats are the last thing that oily-skinned people should include in their diet, EFAs can actually help. Because a diet rich in EFAs supports the cell transference process (which helps to flush the fats and oils that tend to clog pores) and

13

provides a healthy balance of moisture, it can help reduce oiliness.

Food sources: Avocados, cold-pressed coconut oil, extra-virgin olive oil, nuts (especially walnuts, almonds, and macadamias), seeds (pumpkin, sesame, chia, hemp, and flax), spinach

PHOSPHORUS

Phosphorus is the second-most abundant element in the human body. It is involved in hundreds of cellular activities that the skeletal structure and vital organs perform every single day. It's essential to synthesize protein, repair cells and tissues, and develop strong bones and teeth. Phosphorus keeps your metabolism running smoothly, which maintains ideal energy levels. It also reduces stress, which often contributes to and worsens oily skin.

Food sources: Almonds, broccoli, chia seeds, sunflower seeds

POTASSIUM

Potassium is a naturally occurring mineral, the third-most abundant in the body. An essential nutrient used to maintain fluid and electrolyte balance, potassium is vital for good health; it aids proper functioning of the nerves and muscles as well as supports digestive and kidney health. It maintains the electrolyte balance and internal fluids by hydrating the cells from the inside out.

Food sources: Avocados, bananas, broccoli, Brussels sprouts, cantaloupe, coconut water, dates, honeydew melons, leafy greens, mushrooms, sea vegetables (especially dulse)

PROBIOTICS

Derived from Greek, the word *probiotic* literally means "for life." It is used to describe the beneficial bacteria that inhabit the human intestinal tract. Probiotics are really just live bacteria that are growing inside of your gut. Good bacteria can be your best friend: they improve digestion and nutrient absorption, promote glowing skin, and can even elevate your mood. Did you know that 80 percent of your immune system is located in your gut, and 90 percent of your serotonin is produced there too? The foundation of your health, happiness, and beauty lies in your gut! Through eating probiotic-rich fermented foods, you can nurture intestinal microflora, heal your gut, and recolonize your intestines with organisms that defend against disease, viruses, and harmful yeasts.

Food sources: Apple cider vinegar, beet kvass, blue-green algae (such as spirulina), coconut kefir, fermented vegetables (especially sauerkraut, kimchi, and pickles), kombucha, miso paste, raw cheese, yogurt

SELENIUM

Selenium is an essential mineral that functions as an amino acid, neutralizing free radicals and other skin-damaging compounds before they can lead to wrinkles. It is very effective at protecting the skin from sun damage and maintaining its firmness and elasticity. Due to its antioxidant and anti-inflammatory properties, selenium is a powerhouse for calming inflamed, irritated skin and soothing redness and sensitivity. It is also essential for thyroid function.

Food sources: Brazil nuts, coconut water, mushrooms, oats, spinach, sunflower seeds

SULFUR

Sulfur is a nonmetallic element found in our hair, skin, and nails, and it is one of the most effective remedies for acne, rough or oily skin, and clogged pores. It is even known to encourage exfoliation through softening and removing the outermost layer of the skin, which prevents clogged pores and encourages the growth of new skin. Sulfur can also eliminate the bacteria and dead skin cells that clog up pores, attacking the problem that causes acne, eczema, and dandruff at its root.

Food sources: Bee pollen, blue-green algae (such as spirulina), coconut, cruciferous vegetables (such as broccoli, Brussels sprouts, and cauliflower), garlic, hemp seeds, leafy greens (especially arugula, kale, and watercress), maca root, radish (such as black, daikon, and red)

ZINC

Zinc is a vital micronutrient—not only is it one of the most versatile and powerful minerals when it comes to its healing properties, it's also found in every cell of your body. It supports numerous enzymes, boosts the immune system, and helps with wound healing, synthesis of DNA, and normal growth and development. A powerful nutrient, it helps prevent wrinkles, stretch marks, sun damage, inflammation (such as acne and rosacea), and hair loss, and it works synergistically with vitamins to build and repair collagen for smooth, supple skin and strong hair.

Food sources: Blue-green algae (such as spirulina), coconuts, mushrooms, nuts (especially cashews, macadamias, and pine nuts), raw cacao, sea vegetables, seeds (especially pumpkin, sunflower, sesame, and chia), spinach

PART TWO

THE RADIANT PANTRY

VEGETABLES, FRUITS & ROOTS

Nutrient-dense fruits and vegetables are at the heart of almost any radiant recipe. Try visiting your local farmer's market to get inspired by seasonal produce—you will definitely feel the positive effects of eating close to the source.

APPLES

Rich in: Vitamin C, collagen, elastin, and fiber
Eat for: Collagen production, glowing skin, strong and lustrous hair, detoxification

Apples contain an antioxidant known as quercetin (found in the skin of red apples especially) that boosts the immune system to build the natural defenses of the body and lessen the effects of aging and inflammation. Quercetin promotes cellular health and can help stabilize the cells that release histamines in the body, so they have an anti-inflammatory and antihistamine effect. Eating apples can help to prevent hair loss, thanks to their soluble fiber and high concentration of antioxidants, which help increase circulation to the scalp.

ARUGULA

Rich in: Vitamins A, C, and K and calcium
Eat for: Metabolism boost, reduction of undereye circles, cancer fighting, strong bones, DNA protection

The fiber in arugula helps promote digestive regularity, keeping your tummy happy and feeling fuller for longer. Arugula has high levels of chlorophyll, which help to prevent DNA damage. It also helps with the absorption of calcium into the bones and teeth and contains bioactive compounds with anti-inflammatory properties.

ASPARAGUS

Rich in: Vitamins A, B2, C, E, and K, calcium, copper, folate, iron, and potassium
Eat for: Glowing skin, collagen and elastin production, metabolism boost

Asparagus is loaded with folic acid that helps to elevate your mood. Containing high doses of vitamins C and E, this vegetable works magic for skin, nails, and hair by preventing dryness, psoriasis, and blemishes. It is also a powerful detoxifier that cleanses the liver.

AVOCADOS

Rich in: Vitamin K, copper, biotin, folate, good fats, and pantothenic acid
Eat for: Glowing skin, collagen and elastin production, strong and lustrous hair and nails

This creamy, delicious fruit is an amazingly healthy fat. It contains poly- and monounsaturated fatty acids. Monounsaturated fats keep the top layer of skin moist so it's soft and healthy looking. Polyunsaturated fatty acids guard skin from sun damage and protect against symptoms of skin sensitivity and inflammation. Avocados also contain lutein, an antioxidant that promotes hydration and skin elasticity and preserves beneficial skin lipids.

BANANAS

Rich in: Vitamins A, B6, and C, manganese, and potassium
Eat for: Metabolism boost, glowing skin, strong and lustrous hair, beauty sleep, stress relief

Well-known for high concentrations of potassium, bananas are a favorite among athletes for their ability to help relieve muscle cramps, which are a symptom of low potassium levels. Beauty-wise, potassium helps seal in moisture and hydrate the skin, making it soft and supple. It also contains high levels of super-wrinkle-fighting nutrients such as vitamins C and B6, which support the elasticity of the skin, restore natural radiance, and help fade age spots. Meanwhile, the vitamin A in bananas helps to repair dull and damaged skin and restores natural hydration. Bananas also help regulate mood, sleep, and appetite. Remember to choose ripe bananas as their starch has been converted to a much simpler sugar; ripe bananas are much more digestible and nutritious. And don't throw the peel away—it works as an excellent DIY remedy for acne and blemishes: apply the inside of the peel directly onto the problem area to reduce inflammation and destroy bacteria.

BEETS

Rich in: Vitamin C, copper, folate, manganese, and potassium
Eat for: Fighting free radicals, inflammation reduction, detoxification, eye health, glowing skin, antiaging effects, longevity

Beets are a part of the chenopod family, which also includes superfoods like spinach, quinoa, and Swiss chard. This plant family contains unique nutrients that are seldom found in other fruits and vegetables. They are rich in folate, which activates, synthesizes, and repairs DNA. Beets are also a significant source of betalains, which give the root its deep red color. Not only are betalains a powerful antioxidant, but they are anti-inflammatory and detoxifying. They neutralize harmful toxins for safe and efficient elimination and are a wonderfully cleansing food.

BELL PEPPER

Rich in: Vitamins A, B6, and C
Eat for: Collagen and elastin production, anxiety relief, metabolism boost, eye health, strong and lustrous hair, stress relief

All bell peppers are essentially the same type of pepper, but the major factor responsible for the difference in color is how soon the pepper is harvested. In general, a green pepper matures into a yellow, then orange, then red. Because red bell peppers are the ripest, they contain twice the amount of vitamin C than the other colors. Vitamin C is vital for firm, elastic skin and optimal hair growth. Also rich in vitamin A, bell peppers support healthy eyesight, especially night vision. The combination of vitamin B6 and the mineral magnesium helps to alleviate anxiety, particularly as a premenstrual symptom. Being a natural diuretic, vitamin B6 helps to reduce bloating and prevents hypertension. Eat bell peppers raw, as cooking can decrease their benefits by 40 percent.

BLUEBERRIES

Rich in: Vitamins C and K and manganese
Eat for: Fighting free radicals, inflammation reduction, memory boost, eye health, antiaging effects, metabolism boost

Blueberries are not only delicious, but they are an incredible beauty food. They increase your circulation to help give you a more luminous skin. Their deep bluish-purple color results from compounds called anthocyanins—powerful antioxidants that shield the skin against harmful free radicals that can damage collagen. On top of that, blueberries are packed with vitamin C—another antioxidant crucial for collagen production—and they contain resveratrol, which helps reduce sun damage.

BROCCOLI

Rich in: Vitamins C and K, chromium, and folate
Eat for: Antiaging effects, reduction of undereye circles, collagen and elastin production, strong and lustrous hair

Broccoli's high levels of vitamin K help promote healthy blood clotting. Strengthening blood vessels can reduce those pesky dark circles under our eyes and prevent varicose veins. Just one cup of broccoli provides over 270 percent of your daily requirement of vitamin K. It is also very rich in vitamin C, which is essential for collagen and elastin production, and it is a powerful antioxidant defender, regenerating vitamin E in the body.

CARROTS

Rich in: Vitamins A and K and biotin
Eat for: Glowing skin, antiaging effects, UV protection, strong and lustrous hair, eye health

Carrots are actually a member of the parsley family, and their beautiful green shoots are the perfect addition to salads or soups. Packed with nutrients, the most active beauty vitamin here is the powerful A, converted from the beta-carotene that gives carrots their vivid orange color. Vitamin A is crucial for supple, glowing skin, as it protects against ultraviolet damage and helps to repair skin tissue and regulate cellular turnover and collagen production, which is vital for maintaining skin elasticity and preventing wrinkles. Vitamin A is essential for eye health because it protects the surface of the eyes, and a deficiency of this vitamin can lead to a thickening of the cornea and macular degeneration.

CAULIFLOWER

Rich in: Vitamins C and K and folate

Eat for: Antiaging effects, inflammation reduction, detoxification, eye health, metabolism boost, strong and lustrous hair

Known for its cancer-fighting properties, cauliflower is also rich in skin-enhancing nutrients. Cauliflower contains a rich antiaging phytochemical called sulforaphane, a compound known to inhibit the occurrence of some cancers, protect against free-radical damage to DNA, reduce redness caused by sun exposure, lower inflammation, and boost production of antiaging and detoxifying glutathione.

COCONUTS

Rich in: Vitamins C and E, manganese, copper, and iron

Eat for: Antiaging effects, immune system boost, glowing skin

Young coconuts bear a delicious, creamy meat and thirst-quenching, electrolyte-rich water. Not only are coconuts antiviral, antifungal, antibacterial, and antiparasitic, they are also rich in beautifying agents. The mineral balance in coconut water—rich in potassium, magnesium, and sodium, plus small amounts of zinc, copper, and selenium—helps oxygenate the blood efficiently throughout the body, making your skin luminous and supple. Coconut's selenium is an important antiaging mineral that maintains skin elasticity and a healthy scalp, and its zinc keeps hair and nails gorgeous and immunity strong.

CUCUMBERS

Rich in: Vitamins C and K and biotin

Eat for: Collagen production, detoxification, strong and lustrous hair and nails

The greatest and most important skin benefit of the cucumber is its ability to revitalize and hydrate the skin. The presence of beta-carotene helps to fight free radicals, and flavonoids help control skin damage to promote a healthy, inflammation-free complexion. It's a great detoxifier, containing a whopping 90 percent or more of water that hydrates and replenishes the body, and it helps to eliminate toxins by sweeping waste products out of the system. High levels of vitamin K and biotin strengthen bones and support strong hair and nails.

GARLIC

Rich in: Vitamins B6 and C and manganese

Eat for: Glowing skin, strong and lustrous hair, anti-viral action, inflammation reduction

Widely recognized for its therapeutic properties, garlic is also a marvelous beauty food. High in manganese and rich in compounds like allicin, it has antifungal, antiaging, and skin-smoothing benefits. Garlic also enhances blood flow, giving the skin a natural overall glow and stimulating hair growth. Both allicin and sulfur are known to increase collagen

23

production, promoting the skin's elasticity, which helps prevent stretch marks from occurring and reduces wrinkles. Calcium helps combat free radicals that can build up in the skin thus keeping it firm and youthful.

GINGER

Rich in: Vitamin C, magnesium, and potassium
Eat for: Blemish-free skin, inflammation reduction, strong and lustrous hair

Considered an essential medicinal food in China and India, ginger is a soothing, anti-inflammatory root famous for calming upset stomachs and reducing inflammation throughout the body. It also contains an antioxidant called gingerol that not only fights skin-damaging free radicals but also promotes smoothness and evenness in skin tone. Because ginger is energizing and is believed to improved circulation, it is often used in cellulite-reducing treatments and for stimulating hair growth.

KALE

Rich in: Vitamins A, C, and K
Eat for: Detoxification, strong and lustrous hair, collagen production, reduction of undereye circles

Considered the king of leafy greens, kale is actually a member of the Brassica family, making it a close relative to broccoli and Brussels sprouts. Just one cup of raw kale contains over 100 percent of your daily requirements for vitamins A, C, and K, providing phenomenal beauty benefits. It helps to tighten pores, reduce dark undereye circles, promote collagen production, increase cell turnover, prevent free-radical damage, and detoxify the skin. Besides its rich vitamin content, kale is also known to be packed with omega-3 and omega-6 fatty acids, benefiting your hair by promoting elasticity and strengthening the roots. It also improves the blood circulation in your scalp, stimulating hair growth.

LEEK

Rich in: Vitamins A, B6, C, and K and manganese
Eat for: UV protection, reduction of undereye circles, collagen production, detoxification, strong and lustrous hair

Leeks are packed with essential vitamins, minerals, antioxidants, and dietary fiber. Wonderfully rich in the vitamin K that helps get rid of dark circles under the eyes, the green leaves contain one hundred times more beta-carotene and twice as much vitamin C than the white parts, so be sure to use the entire leek. They also have a dietary fiber that acts as a natural prebiotic for gut health when eaten raw. Leeks are rich in collagen-boosting silica and sulfur, which support skin elasticity and healthy hair.

LEMON

Rich in: Vitamin C and folate
Eat for: Collagen production and repair, immune system boost, pH balance

This citrus fruit has amazing antioxidant, antibacterial, antifungal, and astringent properties that help improve the appearance and condition of your skin, hair, and nails. An excellent source of vitamin C, lemons boost collagen production, even out skin tone, and reduce the appearance of age spots. You can even use lemon juice in your hair, as the acidity is brilliant for cleansing both your scalp and hair to remove shampoo and oil buildup and can also reduce dandruff. Although lemons might seem acidic, when eaten they are actually very alkalinizing to the body. Drinking fresh lemon juice in water regularly is one of the best ways to neutralize the body's pH.

OLIVES

Rich in: Vitamin E, copper, fiber, and iron
Eat for: Glowing skin, inflammation reduction, eye health

Believe it or not, olives are an anti-inflammatory antidote to modern ills. Eating them regularly will give your body more access to polyphenols, oleuropein in particular, which is a chemical compound known for its powerful antioxidant, antiatherogenic (preventing fatty deposits in the arteries), anti-inflammatory, antifungal, and antimicrobial properties. They can also help to cut oxidative stress in the brain and boost memory. Due to their high vitamin E content, olives help strengthen your skin's outermost layer to better withstand environmental damage. They also contain hyaluronic acid, which is a great way to plump your skin and make fine lines fade.

ONIONS

Rich in: Vitamins A, B6, C, and E, copper, and manganese
Eat for: Glowing skin, strong nails, lustrous hair, collagen production

This humble vegetable can provide you with glowing skin, thanks to its rich amounts of vitamins A, C, and E, which fight against harmful ultraviolet rays and prevent free-radical damage that can cause premature aging. Onions are one of the richest sources of the pigment quercetin—a powerful antioxidant that can keep your skin wrinkle-free by treating and protecting against ultraviolet damage. They are also rich in vitamin B6, which is essential for strong, healthy nails and hair.

ORANGES

Rich in: Vitamins A and C, fiber, and folate
Eat for: Antiaging effects, glowing skin, collagen and elastin production

One of the most beautifying fruits around, oranges are packed with vitamin C, which stimulates collagen production in the body, helping to reduce wrinkles and sagging skin. Their high calcium content contributes to antioxidant production—reversing dryness and providing the appearance of healthy and glowing skin. Oranges also contain vital nutrients such as bioflavonoids that help stimulate hair growth and strengthen your locks. They also contain folic acid, a type of B vitamin that is vital to hair growth, and high levels of vitamin A that help protect your skin from invading bacteria and viruses.

PAPAYAS
Rich in: Vitamins A, B6, and C and manganese
Eat for: Enzyme boost, collagen production, immune system boost, strong and lustrous hair

Columbus called the papaya the "fruit of the angels." They are loaded with antioxidants that combat free radicals to protect skin cells from damage and reduce fine lines and sagging skin by firming and tightening. Papayas are an abundant source of digestive enzymes that help improve the health of the gut, and they also rejuvenate your complexion by getting rid of dead skin. Extremely rich in vitamins A, B6, and C, one of the best ways to use this beauty nutrient is to apply a simple mask of fresh papaya to the skin and allow it to sit for five to ten minutes; it will work wonders to brighten and soften the skin.

PINEAPPLES
Rich in: Vitamin C, enzymes, and manganese
Eat for: Inflammation reduction, metabolism boost, bone health, eye health, glowing skin, strong and lustrous hair

Pineapples contain bromelain, an anti-inflammatory enzyme that digests protein. Enzymes help to clean the toxic sludge in your system that can dull your complexion, thin your hair, contribute to acne, and lead to premature lines and wrinkles. These enzymes also control the release of a compound called ATP, which provides vital energy to every cell in your body. Because your body utilizes this energy for cell repair to keep your skin glowing, your hair thick and shiny, and your cells regenerated, the absence of available enzymes can disrupt delivery of this all-important, life-sustaining energy.

PITAYAS
Rich in: B vitamins, vitamin C, carotene, and phosphorus
Eat for: Immune system boost, collagen production, DNA protection

More commonly known as dragon fruit, pitaya's bright colors, quirky spikes, and dappled interior make it one of the most unique beauty nutrients. Grown primarily in Central America and Southeast Asia, pitaya is the fruit of a cactus plant. Its edible seeds contain heart-healthy monounsaturated fats and omega-3 fatty acids for reducing inflammation and protecting the skin from sun damage. They are rich in vitamin C, carotene, phosphorus, and B vitamins, which promote everything from DNA repair and collagen production to a strong immune system.

RASPBERRIES
Rich in: Vitamins C and K, manganese, and biotin
Eat for: Collagen production, acne prevention, strong hair and nails, inflammation reduction, immune system boost, glowing skin

This delicate berry is very rich in anthocyanin, a potent antioxidant that lends the beautiful pink-red color to raspberries. Anthocyanins offer protection against free radicals by helping repair damaged cells and promoting the growth of new healthy ones. This well-rounded flavonoid supports the immune system and is recognized for its anti-inflammatory properties and antiviral benefits. The leaves of red raspberries are famous for their skin-tightening properties and astringent qualities for toning the skin, and the easiest way to get these benefits is to drink raspberry leaf tea. In addition, raspberries are rich in biotin—vital for strong hair and nails— as well as vitamin C, which helps to restore radiance and build collagen, and manganese, which helps to promote elasticity and aid in repair. Raspberry seeds contain high amounts of omega-3 and omega-6 fatty acids, which are great for treating skin-related conditions such as eczema.

RED CABBAGE

Rich in: Vitamins A, C, and K and potassium
Eat for: Fighting free radicals, collagen production, reduction of undereye circles, immune system boost, eye health

Red cabbage (also known as purple cabbage) has almost 3,000 times more anthocyanins (an antioxidant) than green cabbage. This antioxidant is what gives red cabbage its beautiful color and helps maintain skin that feels fresh, tight, and flexible. Anthocyanins also reduces wrinkles and age spots.

SHIITAKE MUSHROOMS

Rich in: Vitamins B6 and D, niacin, and pantothenic acid
Eat for: Immune system boost, inflammation reduction, DNA protection, glowing skin, acne prevention

These medicinal mushrooms have been used for thousands of years to treat an array of conditions. They contain many chemical compounds that protect DNA from oxidative damage, helping delay aging and keeping skin looking young and radiant. Shiitakes contain almost all the essential amino acids (lysine and arginine being very abundant), along with a type of essential fatty acid called linoleic acid, which helps with weight loss and muscle building. Packed with antioxidant properties, shiitakes also possess the ability to fight inflammation that affects the skin, so they even help with conditions like rosacea, eczema, and acne.

SPINACH

Rich in: Vitamins A and K, folate, iron, magnesium, and manganese
Eat for: Glowing skin, acne prevention, eye health, inflammation reduction, fighting free radicals, strong and lustrous hair

This age-old superfood is one of the richest sources of vitamin K—a powerhouse for promoting a glowing complexion, minimizing acne and bruising on the skin, and lessening undereye circles. Spinach is also particularly rich in iron, which helps your red blood cells carry oxygen to hair follicles and destroys free radicals in your body, preventing damaged skin and premature aging. Another plus of spinach is that it can help protect your vision: it contains several important phytochemicals, including lutein, which help prevent age-related eye conditions.

STRAWBERRIES

Rich in: Vitamins A and C, folate, and manganese

Eat for: Fighting free radicals, collagen production, inflammation reduction, eye health, glowing skin, UV protection

Strawberries are one of the most nutritious foods available—they are super rich in vitamins A and C and can aid in lowering inflammation, boosting the immune system, and combating oxidative stress. This nutrient-dense fruit helps lock in moisture, stabilizes the secretion of the sebaceous glands, combats wrinkles and discoloration, and helps with elasticity. The high levels of vitamin C also protect from ultraviolet damage and help with inflammatory rashes that can appear on the skin.

SWEET POTATOES

Rich in: Vitamins A, B6, and C, manganese, and copper

Eat for: Nourishing the skin, stress relief, collagen production, UV protection

No food on the planet contains more vitamin A than sweet potatoes! Eating sweet potatoes helps repair cell damage caused by excessive ultraviolet exposure and provides an internal layer of protection from the harmful ultraviolet rays of the sun. Sweet potatoes also contain a good amount of minerals such as magnesium and iron. Magnesium can help you relax and acts as a stress buster for the skin.

SWISS CHARD

Rich in: Vitamins A, C, K, and E, copper, and phytonutrients

Eat for: Reduction of undereye circles and stretch marks, collagen production, fighting free radicals, inflammation reduction, detoxification

This dark leafy green is high in vitamins K and E, carotenoids (super antioxidant) and phosphorus. Chard is one of the richest sources of vitamin K around (one cup has over 600 percent of the recommended daily value). Because both damaged skin and poor circulation can increase the appearance of dark circles, eating foods like Swiss chard that heal and boost the skin's elasticity can lighten the circles under your eyes.

TURMERIC

Rich in: Iron and manganese

Eat for: Glowing skin, acne reduction, elevating mood, detoxification, immune system boost

This medicinal golden root is a close relative of ginger and is best known for its anti-inflammatory health benefits. Curcumin, the active

29

ingredient in turmeric, promotes the healing and brightening of skin, and consuming turmeric regularly aids in skin regeneration—from boosting collagen production and diminishing psoriasis to protecting against free radicals. And for those struggling with inflammatory skin issues, turmeric can soften the symptoms of acne and rosacea, lessen fine lines, and even out wrinkles. Turmeric is also used as a detoxifying agent, helping the liver to flush toxins.

WINTER SQUASH
(ACORN, BUTTERNUT, KABOCHA, PUMPKIN, ETC.)

Rich in: Vitamins A and C, fiber, manganese, and omega-3 fatty acids
Eat for: Fighting free radicals, inflammation reduction, collagen production, glowing skin, UV protection, immune system boost

Thanks to its rich supply of pH-balancing and skin-cell-turnover-boosting vitamin A, squash works wonders for your skin. In one cup of squash you get more than half the daily recommended value of vitamin A. As if that weren't enough, butternut squash also provides UV protection and wrinkle-fighting beta-carotene and vitamin C. Because squash promotes cell turnover, it helps avoid dry, rough, and scaly skin.

GRAINS & GRASSES

Grains are considered one of the most important food staples throughout the world. Nutritionally, grains have a diverse portfolio of proteins, carbohydrates, fiber, vitamins, and minerals. Most whole grains contain fiber and B vitamins. Fiber is essential for digestive and intestinal health; it adds bulk to food, aiding in digestion and elimination. Moreover, fiber stabilizes blood sugar during digestion by regulating nutrients and sugar in the digestive tract. Many grains are also an essential source of vitamin E, a nutritive anti-oxidant that protects cells and tissues from the damaging, age-accelerating free radicals.

Sprouting grains amplifies their nutritional value. Wheat berries sprouted for four days have 30 percent more vitamin E than whole wheat at any other stage in its development or maturity. Often a sensitivity or perceived allergy to wheat is actually the symptom of intolerance to gluten. Generally, grains with less gluten are easier to digest and more nutritious, and sprouting grains makes gluten more digestible. In fact, grains grown fully into grasses have almost none of the gluten found in whole grains.

The sprouting process is a complete biological transformation of the seed. In this process, there is a lessening of the starch of the grain, and at the same time an increase in the protein, fat, amino acid composition, and B vitamin content. The enzymatic action that occurs in the sprouting process also decreases the anti-nutrients that block mineral absorption.

SOAKING

Once widely practiced throughout the cultures of the world, soaking grains is making a comeback, and rightly so. All grains can be soaked, including wheat, buckwheat groats, farro, oats, kamut, quinoa, millet, bulgur, rice, amaranth, and barley. Soaking involves submerging the grains in warm water with an acid medium and soaking them anywhere from 7 to 24 hours depending on the hardness of the grain in order to make them easier to digest.

Grains contain anti-nutrients called phytates, or phytic acid, that bind to important minerals such as zinc, magnesium, and iron. By blocking the absorption of key minerals, they can cause mineral deficiencies that lead to poor bone, dental, and immune health. Although cooking the grains breaks down phytates to a degree, it's not enough to prevent them from influencing mineral levels. That is why soaking grains is such an important step in grain preparation. Soaking grains before cooking activates an enzyme, phytase, that effectively reduces the phytic acid content of the grain, making its minerals available and easy to absorb.

SPROUTING

Ancient ways of harvesting grain allowed the grains to germinate or sprout in the field. Any seed, grain, or bean that has the potential to be a plant is sproutable. This includes lentils, soybeans, mung beans, chickpeas, alfalfa, oats, barley, and peas—just to name a few! And, because most of these ingredients are sold dried, they're readily available for sprouting and inexpensive to buy in bulk. Sprouts can be grown at any time of the year as well, offering a massive variety of powerful plant-based nutrition regardless of the season. Bean sprouts might trigger an allergic reaction in people with peanut allergies.

Amino acids are the building blocks of protein, and they are some of the most important raw materials for your beauty: they're essential for manufacturing healthy hair, nails, skin cells, and collagen, and for repairing them, and they carry out instructions from your DNA to produce healthy beauty essentials like hormones and enzymes. There are nine essential amino acids that our bodies cannot produce. They are referred to as "essential" because they are necessary for the assimilation and formation of protein.

The protein in grains is generally deficient in one or two of the essential amino acids. When a seed is sprouted, most of the nutrients transfer to the shoots, and one of these is protein. Although seeds, grains, and beans are inherently high in protein, sprouting them increases their protein content by between 15 and 30 percent, depending on the plant. The nutrients in sprouted grains are highly bioavailable, or easily absorbed by the body, and the sprouting process increases certain naturally occurring active enzymes, which helps improve digestion and overall immunity.

Here are some simple instructions for sprouting chickpeas. Rinse one cup of dried chickpeas and wash them well. Place them in a quart-size sprouting jar or another sprouting container. Add three cups water, filling the jar until it is about three-quarters full. Cover the jar with a sprouting screen or a mesh sprouting lid. Soak the chickpeas at least eight hours or overnight.

Drain and rinse the chickpeas thoroughly. Invert the jar over a bowl at an angle, so that the chickpeas will drain, but still allow air to circulate through the jar. Repeat this rinsing and draining two to three times per day, tasting the sprouts daily. Discontinue rinsing and draining when the sprouts have reached the desired length and flavor; usually this will take three or four days. Store the sprouts in the refrigerator for up to one week.

FAVORITE GRAINS

These are the grains that I eat the most. They are gluten free, easy to digest, and full of beauty nutrients.

BUCKWHEAT

Buckwheat is considered an alkaline grain. Not technically a cereal grain, it is an edible fruit seed from a spindly plant with heart-shaped leaves. Buckwheat has mildly mucilagenic properties, which makes it easy to digest and soothing to the digestive tract. Rutin, a bioflavonoid found in buckwheat, decreases the formation of wrinkle-promoting AGEs in the body, making buckwheat a major antiaging beauty food. It also helps heal and support capillaries, reduce blood pressure, and stimulate circulation.

Whole buckwheat can be purchased several ways: whole and raw, dehydrated, and toasted. Whole, raw buckwheat groats are a pale beige, and they are perfect for soaking, sprouting, and dehydrating. Dehydrated buckwheat makes delicious raw granola (Tropical Matcha Granola, page 108) and other treats.

OATS

Oats are a gentle and nutritious grain. Very popular as a breakfast cereal, oats can be found in many forms, including oatmeal or rolled oats, steel-cut oats, and whole oat groats. Whole oat groats have an unadulterated nutritional portfolio. Oats are high in silicon, which promotes strength and elasticity in skin and hair and is also important for building collagen and strong connective tissues and to renew bones. Oats are also rich in phosphorus, which is necessary for brain and nerve development, and manganese, which helps maintain healthy hair and hair color and supports mitochondrial health. And don't forget that oats are high in selenium, which promotes skin elasticity and the production of glutathione, the body's master antiaging nutrient. For the most beauty benefits, buy gluten-free oats.

QUINOA

Originally grown in the South American Andes for thousands of years, quinoa is one of the most ancient and nutritious foods around. The Incas called quinoa "the mother grain." Technically not a grain, quinoa is a starchy seed that grows in clusters at the end of a stalk on an annual herb. Naturally gluten free, a serving of this nutrient-dense, energy-building "grain" contains more calcium than milk and more protein than an egg. Unlike most grains, quinoa is a complete protein, meaning it contains all nine essential amino acids that help to build strong, youthful skin, hair, and nails as well as repair daily damage. Quinoa is also full of beauty minerals such as iron, zinc, magnesium, manganese, and phosphorus. Its complex carbohydrates and low glycemic index steady your blood sugar and keep you satiated yet free of bloating. Quinoa also supports healthy digestion with prebiotic fiber that feeds the healthy bacteria in your intestines.

WILD RICE

Wild rice is neither a rice nor a typical grain. It is actually the fruit-seed of a tall aquatic grass indigenous to the Great Lakes and the northern United States and southern Canada. Wild rice is known to have been harvested by Native Americans more than 10,000 years ago.

Rich in vitamins like A, B, C, D, and E, wild rice is an excellent source of beautifying agents for healthy, supple skin and hair. Wild rice has twenty to thirty times more antioxidants than white rice, making it excellent at combating free radicals and contributing to firm skin. If you want to feel younger, add this nutty-flavored rice to your diet.

HERBS

These delicate greens are nutritional powerhouses—full of inflammation-taming, immunity-boosting, detoxifying nutrients. Not only are these plants deeply restorative, but they also add texture, flavor, and an element of beauty to every meal. For an instant boost of beauty nutrition, incorporate a variety of herbs into your juices, smoothies, soups, and salads daily, adding depth, complexity, and flavor.

BASIL

There are few things better than the smell of fresh basil in the summer. In addition to making lovely pesto, vitamin K–rich basil is anti-inflammatory and anti-bacterial. It also contains flavonoids that protect cells from oxidative damage. Eat raw whenever possible so the beneficial oils are still intact.

CILANTRO

Cilantro is loaded with nutritional properties—most notably, its ability to clear toxins, specifically heavy metals. In addition, it can help reduce stress and improve sleep quality. It is also loaded with antioxidants, vitamins A and C, and fiber. Acting as a natural antiseptic and antifungal agent, cilantro is great for treating skin disorders like fungal infections and eczema. Feeling a little bloated? Cilantro is a wonderful overall digestive aid and can also help with nausea.

DILL

Named from the Norwegian word *dilla*, meaning "to lull," dill is sometimes used to induce sleep. Dill has a long, hollow stalk and feathery leaflets like a smaller version of fennel. With a distinctly sweet, sharp flavor, dill is a fantastic source of antioxidants such as beta-carotene. It's also full of calcium, iron, and magnesium, which all help to support bone density. Dill's volatile oils help to neutralize environmental toxins and may protect the body from free radicals.

LAVENDER

These little purple flower buds are excellent for promoting sleep and alleviating anxiety. Lavender also contains antioxidants known as polyphenols that fight belly bloating. Its fragrance is calming, relaxing, and balancing, both physically and emotionally. Therapeutic-grade lavender is great for the skin and can be used to cleanse cuts, bruises, and skin irritations. You can incorporate it into your recipes by grinding the dried flowers or steeping them (Infused Floral Milk, page 81). One of my favorite ways to use lavender is to sprinkle some lavender buds into my ice tea or add them to a refreshing summer-fruit-based juice, ice cream base, cookie or pie dough, or sauce, but remember: a little goes a long way!

LEMONGRASS

Lemongrass contains a wide range of vitamins, minerals, and antioxidants that support glowing, smooth skin and strong hair and nails. When cut, lemongrass has a lovely citrus aroma, and it is widely used to flavor Thai dishes. Lemongrass gains its medicinal properties from a compound called citronella oil, which is commonly used in aromatherapy as well as to ward off pesky mosquitoes! Citronella can help treat and prevent colds, fevers, and headaches, and offers muscular-pain relief as well. In addition, it can alleviate anxiety and reduce stress.

MINT

Mint is great for digestive distress, nausea, headaches, coughing, and fatigue—to name just a few things! Mint is a great source of vitamin A—providing more than half of the recommended daily intake in just two tablespoons—which is essential for cell renewal and the production of new skin cells, membranes, and tissues.

OREGANO

This traditional Greek herb is an amazing immune system booster, which is why it is often referred to as "nature's antibiotic." This powerful herb is antibacterial, antifungal, and anti-inflammatory. It also acts as an antioxidant in the body, preventing damage from toxins on a cellular level while inhibiting the growth of cancer cells and lowering systemic inflammation. Oregano oil is often used to treat upper respiratory infections.

PARSLEY

This game-changing green is a nutritional powerhouse. The most notable health benefits of parsley can be found in its two unique components: volatile oils and flavonoids. The flavonoids in parsley reduce and prevent oxygen-based damage within your blood cells. They contain properties that increase the antioxidant capacity of your blood, which reduces inflammation, slows aging, and protects against ultraviolet damage. The folic acid in parsley comes with even more blood-friendly benefits, helping to control blood pressure to protect your heart, and it repairs cells and synthesizes DNA. Add into the mix that parsley is great for digestion, rich in vitamins A, B12, C, and K (153% of your daily amount), and strengthens your immune and nervous system, and you've got one super-powered little green.

ROSEMARY

This fragrant herb thrives in dry, sunny climates and isn't just ideal for cocktails and soups, it's great for upset stomachs and helps stimulate your digestive and circulatory systems. It is also known to boost mood and memory, in addition to promoting hair growth. Rosemary is an excellent hair tonic; it excels at removing loose scalp flakes and smoothing and strengthening hair strands. It also rejuvenates dry skin and eases the appearance of fine lines.

SAGE

Sage is known as a purifier, which is why it's used in smudge sticks to cleanse the energy in a space. From the family Lamiaceae like most culinary herbs (lavender, mint, rosemary, and others), this antioxidant-packed herb is also wonderful at reducing inflammation everywhere in the body. Research indicates that sage may help improve memory and brain function. With a mildly bitter, astringent flavor and intoxicating aroma, you often find this herb in savory fall dishes.

THYME

Once used for its aromatic qualities by the ancient Greeks in baths and as incense, thyme was believed to bring both courage and protection to those who used it. Today its uses have expanded, as it has proven beneficial for fighting sore throats, lowering blood pressure, preventing food poisoning, and elevating mood. This herb has long been used as an herbal remedy for respiratory problems, such as bronchitis, whooping cough, and sore throats. Thyme contains a unique volatile oil called thymol, a naturally occurring compound that can destroy harmful organisms and is used as an antiseptic.

SPICES & ACCENTS

Good-quality seasonings are just as important as good ingredients: They enhance flavors and add depth without overpowering the food. A simple dusting of a spice or seasoning can completely transform a dish, and better yet, so many of the most flavorful ones are also good for you. You'll want to have an assortment on hand so that your pantry is stocked full of these simple ways to add layers of complexity to any dish.

APPLE CIDER VINEGAR

This amazing healing elixir has a high probiotic content and is great for alkalinizing the body. It stimulates the natural production of hydrochloric acid in the stomach, which is essential for proper digestion and metabolic function, which leads to healthy, glowing skin. In addition, apple cider vinegar has been shown to improve blood sugar levels, aiding in natural weight loss, and to reduce inflammation and pain in the body. This energizing, cleansing, healing beauty food is perfect to use as a seasoning, for marinades, and to complement strong flavors. Be sure to buy raw, unrefined apple cider vinegar "with the mother" (that is, the beneficial bacteria and enzymes) to get the most potent beauty benefits.

BLACK PEPPER

If freshly ground, this warming, aromatic spice boosts the immune system, aids digestion, stimulates blood flow, and supports the liver's detoxification process. I love to add it to sweet milks alongside chai spices such as cardamom and ginger, and I find that it is perfect for finishing a dish—offering that extra touch that brings everything together.

BRAGG LIQUID AMINOS

Amino acids are the building blocks of our cells. They are the link between our food and our bodily tissues. Essential for beauty, they produce and repair hair, nails, skin cells, and collagen, and they also carry out instructions from your DNA to produce healthy hormones and enzymes. I love to use Liquid Aminos as a healthy, gluten-free alternative to soy sauce.

CARDAMOM

A favorite of Ayurvedic medicine, cardamom is the perfect spice for cold and flu season. It is one of the richest sources of the phytochemical eucalyptol, which is a potent antiseptic. It can be used to fight off sore throats, and it breaks up chest congestion, making it a remedy for bronchitis, laryngitis, and any type of upper-respiratory infection. My favorite spice by far, I add it to everything from desserts (Blueberry Acai Crumble, page 237) to savory dishes (Moroccan Spiced Bowl with Rainbow Quinoa, page 225, to drinks (Invincible Coffee, page 78).

41

CAYENNE

This fiery red spice is used worldwide to add flavor to meals and turn up the heat. Cayenne is a spicy metabolic stimulant that aids in detoxification and helps activate blood circulation—supporting full-system cleansing and radiance. Capsaicin, the active ingredient in cayenne, has long been linked to increasing metabolic function and aiding in weight loss. Additionally, it may help to reduce appetite and improve circulation.

CINNAMON

This nourishing spice is like a warm blanket on cold days. Not only does it bring warmth to both sweet and savory dishes, it also aids in lowering blood sugar, preventing the insulin spikes that lead to wrinkles and blemishes. Used for centuries to stimulate circulation and digestion, to boost overall vitality, and for its antiseptic properties, cinnamon also contains iron, calcium, manganese, and potent antioxidants that are linked to fighting inflammation and lowering cholesterol.

MESQUITE

Used as a medicinal food in some Native American cultures, mesquite is nutrient rich, with high levels of calcium, potassium, and zinc. Mesquite pods are ground into a fine powder that is sweet and a great substitute for sugar in desserts. Its malty, caramel flavor is both decadent and low glycemic, aiding in sugar metabolism. Mesquite powder can be used to build and maintain strong bones and teeth, to support the cardiovascular and immune system, and to enhance athletic performance. It is also rich in soluble fiber, making it an important player in normalizing bowels, controlling cholesterol levels, and clearing the body of toxic waste.

MISO

This salty, savory, fermented paste is rich in B vitamins, live enzymes, protein, and good bacteria. Commonly made of soybeans, rice, or barley, you can also find miso made from chickpeas, adzuki beans, or millet. Generally, darker miso indicates a longer fermentation period and a stronger flavor. The lighter the miso, the mellower and sweeter the flavor. Use miso to season soups or stews—similar to bouillon or soy sauce—and as a salty thickener in sauces. It's very important not to overheat miso or let it boil, or it will lose many of its beneficial properties. Be sure to look for misos that are naturally fermented and unpasteurized.

NUTRITIONAL YEAST

Nutritional yeast is an excellent source of B vitamins, particularly B12, which is missing from many vegan and vegetarian diets. This vital nutrient is needed to help speed up reactions in your body, and deficiency can cause anemia and nervous system damage. Nutritional yeast is a great source of all eighteen amino acids. It is also rich in fifteen minerals including iron, magnesium, phosphorus, zinc, chromium, and selenium. Anyone can benefit from adding these crumbled flakes to their diet, and this magic powder gives a nutty, cheesy flavor to any dish (such as Beet Raviolis with Basil Ricotta, page 196).

PINK SALT

Pink salt is an unrefined salt that comes from naturally formed sea and mountain beds. Commonly found in the Himalayas, the Mediterranean, and the Hawaiian Islands, this amazing salt contains over ninety health-promoting trace minerals, including phosphorus, bromine, boron, zinc, iron, manganese, copper, and silicon. Pink salt is an important source of hydrochloric acid, which is used by the stomach to digest foods properly, preventing the onslaught of a host of issues such as acne, fatigue, and bloating. It works as an electrolyte, balancing the fluid both inside and outside your body's cell walls. Pink salt also helps to alkalize the body, improve digestion, boost energy, and nourish the skin.

ROSE WATER

Consumed for centuries for health and beauty benefits, rose water is steam-distilled from organic roses. Add it to water, a hot or cold drink (Rose Quartz Latte, page 93), a dressing, or a dessert for a delicate sweetness. It's cooling to the body, soothing to the heart and mind in stressful situations, and an aphrodisiac, and it also supports the metabolism and the digestive tract. Rose water can be used as a refreshing tonic for the face as well: spritz it on the skin a couple times a day to hydrate and revitalize your skin.

SUN-DRIED TOMATOES

Sun-dried tomatoes are a flavorful addition to many dishes and sauces. Like raw tomatoes, the sun-dried variety are full of antioxidants, vitamins, and beauty minerals. The nutritional profile of tomatoes declines rapidly after they are picked due to their high moisture content, but drying helps preserve these amazing nutrients while retaining and concentrating their beautiful flavor. Sun-dried tomatoes contain high levels of the antioxidant lycopene, which helps defend against ultraviolet damage. These dried varieties can be stored indefinitely in a cool, dry place, and you can rehydrate them whenever needed: In a heatproof bowl, cover the sun-dried tomatoes with warm water and let them stand for ten minutes or until they are easily pierced with a fork. Marinated sun-dried tomatoes can also be purchased in a jar. (Be mindful of the ingredients, though, as most manufacturers use inorganic oils and sneak in preservatives.)

TAMARI

A premium form of Japanese soy sauce made with just fermented soybeans, tamari is often gluten free, but always check the label. I use it often; just a few drops can transform a plain, boring dish into something extraordinary.

43

UMEBOSHI PLUM VINEGAR

Prized for its alkalizing benefits, this vinegar is the brine from pickling umeboshi plums. A popular seasoning in Japan, China, and Korea, it is also used as a medicinal remedy: its sour, salty, and sweet flavors are believed to combat fatigue, stimulate digestion, and promote the elimination of toxins. An excellent vinegar with balanced acidity, it is perfect for salads, dressings, sauces, and dips. Make sure to buy umeboshi vinegar that is naturally fermented and additive free. You can find this ingredient in any health food store. It serves as a savory flavor base for macrobiotic and Japanese cooking.

VANILLA

Known as an ancient aphrodisiac, vanilla is an antioxidant that soothes the nervous system and alleviates stress. I only use ground raw vanilla beans because they have the most exquisite flavor. I love to add vanilla to desserts and sweet beverages for a subtle richness.

TRANSFORMATIONAL FOODS

These medicinal plant-based foods are packed with exceptionally high levels of vitamins, minerals, antioxidants, and enzymes. You can use these amazing foods to beautify, nourish, tone, and empower your body every day. They can heal your cells, protect against oxidation, and slow the aging process by stimulating and supplementing your body's immune system. Add them to your morning smoothie, sprinkle them over soup, or use them in raw treats for daily transformation.

ACAI

Acai is a small, dark purple berry that grows on the acai palm in the Amazon forest of Brazil. The nutrients come from the pulp and skin of the fruit, and the berries taste like a mix of blueberries and chocolate. Used for its beautifying abilities, acai berries are extremely high in antioxidants, which help eliminate free radicals. They are also rich in B vitamins, vitamins C and K, zinc, calcium, iron, potassium, and manganese. It increases overall blood circulation of the body, which may also contribute to a boost in sex drive (especially for men). Acai is available in frozen packs, whole frozen berries, and powder. Always opt for the unsweetened variety.

ASHWAGANDHA

This mineral-dense adaptogen aids the thyroid, soothes anxiety, relieves stress, improves sleep, and contributes to virility. Widely used in Ayurveda, it is considered to be the best rejuvenative herb. It is said to give the user the stamina and strength of a stallion (in Hindi, *asgandh* means "horse sweat"). In Ayurvedic medicine, it is considered a "rasayana" herb. (Rasayana is one of the eight specialized branches of the practice of Ayurveda, and it deals with the maintenance of health. *Rasa*, meaning juice or fluid, is the vital fluid that we extract from the food we eat. It brings nourishment, carries off toxins, and enhances our immunity.) Most adaptogens have a stimulating effect, but ashwagandha is unusual in that it is a calming adaptogen. It enhances endocrine function, especially helping to reregulate thyroid and adrenal glands. Because of its nervine and adaptogen functions, ashwagandha is very effective for alleviating anxiety, fatigue, and cloudy thinking. Interestingly, the "som" in its Latin name—*Withania somnifera*—means "to sleep," and it is in fact a calming plant. The part of the plant used to make this powder is an extract of the root and the leaf.

BEE POLLEN

These tiny pollen granules are one of the most nourishing foods on the planet. Collected and revered by many cultures throughout history, bee pollen is considered a powerful longevity-boosting, antiaging superfood.

Pollen is a complex and nutrition-dense food that includes antioxidants, minerals, and vitamins, along with twenty-two amino acids and bioavailable proteins that support growing lustrous hair and strong nails and aid in the production of new skin cells. Bee pollen's high levels of vitamin B combat acne and wrinkles, nourishing both beauty and energy. A potent aphrodisiac, blood builder, and muscle food, bee pollen supports fertility and stamina, muscle growth and definition, and recovery from exercise. Sprinkle a small amount of bee pollen into smoothies and onto salads and desserts.

BLUE-GREEN ALGAE

One of the most nutrient-dense foods on the planet, blue-green algae grows in freshwater lakes and ponds around the world. Used as a primary source of protein by ancient Aztec and African populations, this green or blue powder contains all of the essential amino acids as well as most of the nonessential amino acids, making it a complete protein supplement. The richest source of the essential acid gamma-linolenic acid (GLA) after human milk, it is amazing for your skin. This algae energizes, alkalizes, and deeply mineralizes, and it soothes inflammation and boosts immunity. A little goes a long way, so start with ¼ teaspoon and move up from there.

CACAO

In their raw state, dried cacao beans are filled with nutrients and health benefits. This South American seed is harvested from the fruit pod of an evergreen tree, and it is at the core of many well-loved (chocolate) desserts. However, cacao has actually been used for centuries in Central and South America for its healing and energizing properties. As a beauty food, cacao is one of the richest in antioxidants—neutralizing free radicals and promoting supple skin. In its raw state, cacao raises levels of tryptophan and therefore serotonin, which is the neurotransmitter that releases mood-boosting endorphins and provides a sense of calm throughout the body. Manganese and iron oxygenate the blood, while magnesium balances brain chemistry and sulfur builds strong nails, hair, and skin. But don't be fooled: these benefits are only active in cacao's raw (dried) form, so look for raw cacao powder and nibs.

CHAGA

Chaga is a wild mushroom that usually grows out of birch trees and survives harsh temperatures by taking its nutrients from the tree itself. Chaga is more nutrient-dense than any of the true mushroom species, and it has a DNA structure that is 30 percent more like a human than a plant. Chaga promotes longevity, slows the aging process, fights inflammatory conditions, and prevents the onset of degenerative diseases. One of the richest sources of the enzyme SOD (superoxide dismutase), an antioxidant that prevents damage to the cell's DNA and oxidation, chaga can help to slow down the aging process and support glowing skin, eyes, and hair. It also possesses antiviral properties, boosts immunity, and balances blood sugar. For the recipes in this book, powdered chaga will work best.

CORDYCEPS

Cordyceps mushrooms increase libido, stamina, and mental energy, and can alleviate stress and promote overall longevity. In traditional Chinese medicine, cordyceps are widely used for strengthening the "kidney" functions, which include brain power, skeletal structural integrity, and harnessing power and motivation. Cordyceps mushrooms also increase cellular oxygen absorption and boost the immune system, and can make for a powerful anti-inflammatory tonic for strength, energy, and lung and brain function as well. The powdered version of this adaptogen will work best to add easily to recipes.

HE SHOU WU

He shou wu is an herb that has been used for centuries as an antiaging, blood-building, beauty, and rejuvenating food with antioxidant polyphenols. Famous for its ability to stimulate hair growth and get rid of gray hair, this herb is also wonderful for balancing hormones, improving adrenal function, and nourishing the skin for an overall glow. An excellent source of iron and zinc, it is believed to raise the SOD levels in the body, which assist in clearing free radicals from the system, making for a deeply restorative tonic.

LUCUMA

Lucuma is a low-glycemic Peruvian superfruit. It provides fourteen essential trace elements, including a considerable amount of iron, potassium, sodium, calcium, magnesium, and phosphorus. It has powerful anti-inflammatory effects, significantly increasing wound closure and promoting tissue regeneration.

Lucuma is dehydrated and then milled into a fine powder, and its distinctive sweet and caramel taste makes it the perfect natural sweetener for elixirs, smoothies, and raw desserts without increasing your blood sugar levels.

MACA

This Peruvian root grows high in the Andes Mountains and is a powerful adaptogen that counters the negative effects of tension and anxiety while toning and balancing the endocrine system. You can find maca root in powdered form. Loaded with amino acids, vitamins B, B1, B2, C, D, and E, as well as fiber and essential fatty acids, this amazing root provides an all-natural energy boost, elevates mental stamina, helps to balance hormones, and enhances libido. It is also known to aid in reproductive function and to boost sex drive. Maca has a nutty and complex caramel flavor that goes well in smoothies and raw desserts.

MATCHA

This silky green tea powder was traditionally used in Japan for tea ceremonies and by Buddhist monks to keep them alert and focused during long days of meditation. Matcha is known for boosting the metabolism, calming anxiety, and cleansing the body. It is rich in blood-oxygenating chlorophyll, a powerful detoxifier, and has one of the highest sources of antioxidants. Matcha is also rich in L-theanine, a rare amino acid that promotes a state of relaxation and well-being. Because it is so rich in chlorophyll and has alkalizing and cleansing benefits, I love to drink matcha several times a week.

MUCUNA PRURIENS

Mucuna pruriens is a tropical vine. In Ayurvedic medicine, mucuna is used as a nerve tonic and adaptogen that helps the body deal with stress. The part used is the seed and it can be found in a powdered form. It is an amazing source of the amino acid L-dopa, a precursor to dopamine, which is a powerful neurotransmitter that elevates your mood, alertness, sex drive, and creativity while soothing the nervous system overall.

PEARL POWDER

Believe it or not, pearls are also a powerful transformational food, having been used in traditional Chinese and Ayurvedic medicine for centuries to promote radiant skin. Pearl powder is made from freshwater pearls or salt-water pearls that are below jewelry grade. In powdered form, pearls stimulate SOD, an antioxidant that help fade blemishes, reduce wrinkles and scarring, and even eliminate the occasional pimple. Rich in calcium, magnesium, iron, silica, and amino acids, pearl powder can help maintain strong bones and teeth and even help prevent osteoporosis. In Chinese medicine, it is also known as a powerful *shen* (spirit) stabilizer, supporting mood stability with its soothing and calming nature. Adding a pinch of pearl powder to your daily tonic can help relieve anxiety and tension associated with occasional stress, promoting calm and well-being.

PROBIOTICS

There are billions of these beneficial microflora living in the intestines and on your skin that are important for digestion and the absorption of vital nutrients that nourish skin, hair, and nails. Having a healthy gut will reward you with increased energy, elevated mood, glowing skin, and stronger immunity. 80 percent of your entire immune system is located in your digestive tract! Protecting the skin internally this way will prevent the onslaught of wrinkles, eczema, blemishes, and premature aging. By taking probiotics to maintain a balance of bacteria in your digestive system, not only will you improve your outer appearance, but you may also prevent digestive problems and other health concerns.

REISHI

One of the most popular transformational foods, reishi is a medicinal mushroom that has been revered in Chinese medicine as the "mushroom of immortality" or "herb of spiritual potency" for over 3,000 years. A potent adaptogen, it helps to create a sense of calm while promoting longevity and nourishing our *shen*, or spiritual energy. Well-known as an immune-boosting herb, reishi is a great supplement you can buy in powdered form to provide overall support, especially if you are feeling stressed and run down.

SCHISANDRA BERRY

Schisandra is perhaps the most beautifying herb of all. This little red berry that grows in northern China and Russia is known in Chinese medicine as the "herb that does it all." Schisandra helps purify the blood while supporting strong memory function and a healthy libido. Take schisandra daily to dramatically improve your skin: due to the astringent quality of schisandra, your skin will retain moisture, which reduces the appearance of fine lines and creates a youthful glow. You can find the fruit or the seed, but the recipes in this book call for the powdered form.

SEA VEGETABLES

These beautiful sea plants are true superfoods that nourish from the inside out. They have mineral profiles nearly identical to our own, and are extremely rich in bioavailable iron for strong, healthy hair and nails, calcium to nourish bones and teeth, and iodine to boost the metabolism and balance hormones. Sea vegetables are rich in collagen-building zinc, as well as iodine and copper, which helps to combat dryness and increase your skin's elasticity. Hijiki, kelp, nori, wakame, arame, kombu, dulse, and agar are my favorites.

NUTS & SEEDS

Nuts and seeds are little storehouses of healthy fats, protein, and beauty minerals that tame inflammation, boost your energy, and deeply mineralize. Rich in anti-inflammatory omega-3 and omega-6 fatty acids, nuts and seeds strengthen the cell membranes, aid in healthy oil production, smooth hydrated skin, boost metabolism and brain function—all while regulating our moods and hormones. They are the perfect finishing touch for salads or quick snack. I use them in everything from creamy dressings (Green Goddess Dressing, page 136) to delicious desserts (Macadamia Shortbread & Salted Caramel Bars, page 242).

Always use raw, unpasteurized nuts and seeds, and don't forget to soak them for a couple of hours or overnight to "activate" them. This allows them to release their enzyme inhibitors so that they are easier to digest and increases their nutritional value. The best way to find the best nuts is to buy organic ones directly from farmers at the farmers' market or online. When recipes call for nut butters, always opt for the raw, unroasted ones, including for tahini.

SOAKING NUTS & SEEDS

To soak two cups raw, unpasteurized nuts and seeds, you'll need enough warm filtered water to cover them and one tablespoon of pink salt. The warm water will neutralize many of the enzyme inhibitors and increase the bioavailability of beauty nutrients, especially B vitamins. The salt will help activate enzymes present in nuts and seeds. (When soaking grains or beans, a more acidic substance is often used, but since nuts and seeds contain less phytic acid than grains/legumes but more enzyme inhibitors, the salt is more beneficial.)

Put the warm water in a medium bowl or jar that is a half gallon or larger. Add the salt and stir until it dissolves. Add the nuts or seeds, making sure they are completely submerged in the water. Leave the bowl uncovered on the counter for at least six or up to twenty-four hours. If you are soaking them in a very warm place, move the bowl to the fridge so the nuts or seeds don't get sour. Seeds usually take less time, around six hours, and hard nuts like almonds and hazelnuts will benefit from a whole day of soaking.

After soaking, rinse the nuts or seeds really well. You can store soaked nuts in the freezer, dehydrate them, or use them right away!

ALMONDS
Almonds are super rich in biotin, a powerful nutrient for hair and nails that also nourishes the adrenals and balances metabolism. They are also a rich source of vitamin E, essential for healthy, glowing skin, optimal immune function, and protection from oxidative damage. Almonds contain magnesium,

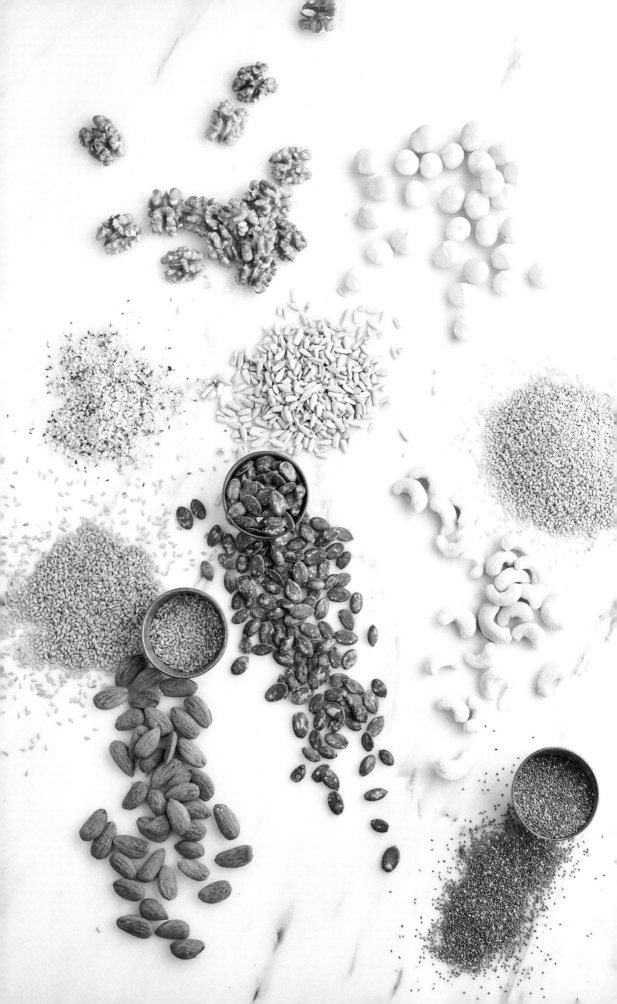

calcium, and folate and are high in monounsaturated fat (the type found in olive oil)—all of which work together to keep the skin moist and healthy, protect it against ultraviolet damage, reduce inflammation, and lower the risk of heart disease.

CASHEWS

This delicately flavored and versatile nut is brimming with minerals and good fats, and it is particularly great for the skin, brain, bones, and nervous system function. Cashews are rich in copper, which assists in the production of collagen while supporting healthy skin, hair, and nails, and magnesium, which helps regulate muscle and nerve function as well as blood sugar and also aids detoxification pathways, including the skin. This creamy nut is also very versatile, able to be transformed into cheese, cream sauce, milk, and more.

CHIA SEEDS

Chia seeds come from the chia plant, which is part of the mint family, Lamiaceae. Native to South America, there's evidence that these seeds were used as early as the 1500s by Aztec tribes. *Chia* means "strength" in ancient Mayan, and the seeds are thought to have been used to increase stamina and endurance. They pack an amazing nutritional punch. Rich in fiber, they can improve elimination and reduce bloating while at the same time making you feel fuller with fewer calories. Chia is a complete protein, crucial for growing strong collagen, elastin, and keratin—the components of youthful skin, hair, and nails. A good source of calcium for strong teeth, bones, and nails, chia is also very high in wrinkle-fighting antioxidants. For a healthy glow, add chia seeds to your beauty pantry.

FLAXSEEDS

Flax is one of the best sources of fat-burning, collagen-boosting omega-3 fatty acids and lignans (believed to help reduce the risk of hormone-related cancers). Rich in nutrients that ensure your skin retains moisture, it contains soluble fiber for healthy elimination and protein to repair skin damage. In order for our bodies to reap their healthy benefits, the seeds must be ground before consuming. Be sure to store in the freezer or refrigerator, as they can quickly become rancid at room temperature.

HEMP SEEDS

A potent source of plant protein, hemp seeds contain twenty amino acids, including the nine essential amino acids our bodies can't produce. This makes hemp one of the most complete plant-based sources of protein available. One ounce of hemp seeds packs in about ten grams of protein. Hemp seeds are also a rich and balanced source of omega-3 and omega-6 fatty acids, which the body needs for energy production, nervous system function, skin health, brain development, immune system support, and cardiovascular health. In addition to the omega fatty acids, hemp seeds and oil contain some fats that are even more difficult to find, such as GLA (gamma-linoleic acid), which can tame inflammation and contribute to smooth, glowing skin and strong hair and nails. Their complex, nutty flavor complements both savory and sweet foods.

MACADAMIA NUTS

Macadamia nuts are originally from Australia, but today, Hawaii is the world's largest grower. Housed in an extremely tough shell is a sweet, rich, marble-sized white nut that contains the perfect one-to-one ratio of essential fatty acids, making it great for heart health. Macadamias are one of the highest sources of palmitoleic fatty acids—vital for delaying aging. Oleic acid is a moisturizing anti-inflammatory, perfect for dry, sensitive skin types. Linoleic acid restores the skin's barrier function and keeps skin hydrated. I love to use these creamy nuts in desserts (Passion Fruit Tart, page 232).

PUMPKIN SEEDS

Pumpkin seeds have long been valued as a source of the mineral zinc—crucial for collagen formation and tissue healing. Containing diverse forms of vitamin E, they help regulate oil production and fight inflammation and redness for blemish-free skin. They also protect against free-radical damage and support healthy levels of antiaging glutathione.

SESAME SEEDS

Sesame seeds have been a food staple for thousands of years, particularly in the Middle East. Sesame is a great source of beautifying minerals including copper, manganese, magnesium, calcium, phosphorus, iron, zinc, molybdenum, and selenium. But best of all, sesame seeds are rich in the natural antioxidant CoQ10, which protects mitochondria from oxidative damage, keeping cell membranes strong and helping to provide energy to cells, and also defends against chronic fatigue and heart conditions.

SUNFLOWER SEEDS

These sweet, nutty seeds are one of nature's greatest sources of vitamin E. They are also high in B vitamins, copper, selenium, magnesium, and phosphorus—all nutrients vital for skin elasticity and protection from free-radical damage.

WALNUTS

Raw walnuts are full of beautifying fats, proteins, and minerals that help hydrate and strengthen your skin and hair. They're one of the few plant sources of skin-strengthening omega-3 fatty acids, which support brain function and help reduce inflammation. Walnuts are rich source of zinc for healthy skin and scalp and calming magnesium, and they contain hard-to-find antioxidant and anti-inflammatory phytochemicals as well as vitamin E, which protects cells and tissues from the damaging, age-accelerating free radicals.

53

SWEETENERS

One of the most important steps for slowing down the aging process is eliminating white sugar from your diet. White sugar and other highly refined sweeteners are chemically processed and contribute to a host of diseases. They contain no nutritional value, and digesting them causes the body to draw on its own reserves of vitamins and minerals, which ultimately leads to a number of deficiencies. Refined sweeteners actively age you by speeding up the degradation of the key skin proteins elastin and collagen. The key is to substitute refined sugars with natural, unrefined sweeteners that have deep, rounded, and complex flavors. The following natural sweeteners contain some beauty nutrients and a lower glycemic index than white sugar, but they should still be eaten in moderation.

COCONUT NECTAR AND SUGAR

This low-glycemic nectar is hand-harvested from coconut blossoms and then evaporated or boiled to thicken it and make coconut nectar. The syrup can then be dehydrated and ground to make coconut sugar. Coconut nectar and sugar are high in potassium, iron, zinc, and vitamins B and C, and when produced at low temperatures they also contain active digestive enzymes.

DRIED DATES

This fruit is a powerhouse of beauty nutrients. Rich in potassium to keep your body hydrated and fiber to help improve elimination and reduce bloating, they also provide calcium, zinc, iron, copper, magnesium, calcium, and other minerals. Although dates are high in sugar, they have a low glycemic index. Their dense, caramel sweetness enriches sweet recipes, and when ground into a paste they are a natural binder for raw treats. If the dates feel too dry, soak them for ten minutes to soften. Medjool dates are by far my favorite variety; they are gooey, and their caramel flavor makes them perfect for recipes such as Acai Beauty Bars (page 110).

MAPLE SYRUP

The boiled-down sap of the sugar maple tree, maple syrup has a mild caramel flavor perfect for making desserts. Pure maple syrup is an outstanding source of manganese, which helps maintain healthy hair and hair color and supports mitochondrial health. It also contains calcium, potassium, and zinc. Incredible as it may seem, pure maple syrup is rich in antioxidants that help neutralize free radicals and reduce oxidative damage. Always go for the darker maple syrups, as they contain more beneficial antioxidants than the lighter syrups.

RAW HONEY

The difference between raw and regular honey is that raw honey hasn't been processed, heated, or pasteurized, so it retains all of its beneficial nutrients.

Raw honey is creamier and thicker, and it is incredibly healing. Packed with beauty nutrients, antioxidants, probiotics, antibacterial properties, and live enzymes, this is my sweetener of choice for milks and tonics. It is also wonderful to use as a hydrating face mask: Just apply a tablespoon to clean skin and rinse after ten to fifteen minutes.

STEVIA

Native to South America, this plant has been used for centuries to treat diabetes and hypoglycemia. Its sweetness comes from the leaves, which are crushed or distilled to create a powder or liquid extract. Stevia is several hundred times sweeter than sugar, has no calories, and may actually improve insulin sensitivity. Because it is so much sweeter than sugar, you only need to use a fraction of the amount. The ratios are as follows: one cup sugar is the equivalent of about one teaspoon stevia. It does leave a bit of an aftertaste, so it's better to combine with other sweeteners.

It is important to differentiate between processed forms of stevia and the naturally occurring herbal form. In the dried leaf or tincture form, it is considered safe and has even been studied and found to have health benefits. Powdered and bleached stevia should not be used because it undergoes an extensive chemical process to reach its final white powdered form. Always opt for stevia in leaf form, or tinctures made from leaf form, but avoid the white processed and powdered versions. A good brand to use is Omnica Organic Liquid Stevia, as it's pure and has no aftertaste.

FATS

We now know that fats can actually be good for you, and that we need good fat for proper brain function, hormone production, energy, immune function, and even weight loss. But don't be fooled into thinking that all fats are created equal. Different fats have different effects on our bodies, and it's crucial to know the hierarchy of fats for a healthy body and mind. It is also important to know which fats to avoid heating, as some can release free radicals that contribute to wrinkles, inflammation, and age spots and create unnecessary acidity in the body. Your brain is 60 percent fat: you will notice that by feeding your brain with much-needed healthy fats, you will feel the mental clarity that enables you to live a healthy, happy, inspired life.

Two fundamental fatty acids you want to look for are omega-3s and omega-6s. Your body doesn't produce these fats, so it's vital that you get them through your food. When not balanced properly with omega-3s, omega-6s can cause problems and inflammation, a contributing factor in dryness, itching, pain, and even weight gain and depression. Raw plant fats like avocado, coconuts, nuts, seeds, ghee, and extra-virgin olive oil are extremely beautifying—keeping your cells healthy and hydrated on the inside and helping to prevent dry skin on the outside. They also energize you, boost your brain power, support your nervous system, and build your immunity. Here are a few of the healthiest fats to have on hand.

COCONUT OIL

Coconut oil has emerged over the years as a superfood with an amazing array of benefits. With its unique combination of fatty acids, antioxidants, and anti-inflammatory properties, coconut oil can be used for just about everything. You can use it to cook at high heat (without oxidizing) as well as for a gentle makeup remover, teeth whitener, diaper-rash treatment, or hair conditioner.

Coconut oil is made of anti-inflammatory, medium-chain fatty acids that burn quickly and easily in the body without being broken down by the liver, providing instant energy and a metabolism boost that actually helps you burn stored fat. The main component of coconut oil is lauric acid, a powerful antimicrobial fat that kills bacteria, viruses, and yeast (it's also found in breast milk!). Lauric acid boosts immunity and supports healthy brain function. Don't worry if your coconut oil has a life of its own: one day it's solid and the next day it's liquid. It is a saturated fat, so it's solid at colder temperatures and melts in warmer conditions. To accurately measure coconut oil for cooking, always measure it in its melted form.

COCONUT BUTTER

Coconut butter is a combination of the meat and oil from the coconut, and it is in the form of a thick paste. It has the same benefits as coconut oil with the added bonus of fiber: one tablespoon of coconut butter provides two

57

grams of fiber as well as small amounts of potassium, magnesium, and iron. It's perfect for enriching desserts or eating by the spoonful.

EXTRA-VIRGIN OLIVE OIL

This fruity oil is particularly rich in vitamin E, which is wonderful for ultraviolet protection and for strengthening cell membranes. Extra-virgin olive oil is best eaten in its raw state, because it is one of the oils that can oxidize during cooking. Use it in salad dressings, to emulsify sauces, and to thicken soups. A natural anti-inflammatory, olive oil is great for calming sensitive skin and is rich in antioxidants that keep your skin looking supple and youthful.

GHEE

Ghee is made by simmering pure sweet cream butter and skimming out the milk solids until the water completely evaporates and only the pure fat remains. It's a close cousin of clarified butter, but it's cooked longer, resulting in a deeper, nuttier flavor. Even though it's shelf-stable and doesn't need to be refrigerated, I like to refrigerate my ghee just because I like the way it melts into my warm drinks.

Ghee is considered a "good" fat because it's rich in medium-chain triglycerides, or MCT. These fatty acids are absorbed quickly by the body, making them a good source of energy, and they have been linked to benefits like decreased hunger, increased metabolism, and weight loss. It's also rich in butyric acid—a short-chain fatty acid that is anti-inflammatory and an essential component of strong immune and digestive systems—as well as linoleic acid and vitamins A, D, E, and K.

Ghee makes a wonderful cooking oil because it will withstand an unusually high temperature, but my favorite application is to add a teaspoon to tea or any warm drink with a dusting of cardamom and a touch of honey for a restorative treat.

NUTS AND SEEDS

Hemp, almond, pumpkin, flax, cashew, sesame, hazelnut, walnut, macadamia, and chia—all of them are wonderful sources of healthy fats. Nuts and seeds are rich in anti-inflammatory, antiaging omega-3 fatty acids and omega-6s and can be transformed into milks and cheeses (Homemade Nut Cheeses & Crackers, page 172), used in crusts or cookies (Matcha Raw-eos, page 245), or simply sprinkled over salads.

TOASTED SESAME OIL

Toasted sesame oil is an amazing addition to Asian-inspired dishes. I love to use it in marinades and dressings, and to bring a delectable accent to sea broth (Nourishing Sea Broth, page 131). It's a nourishing, healthy fat that is particularly high in zinc and vitamin E, which helps your skin look younger for longer. A little goes a long way, so be careful to add a little at a time.

EQUIPMENT

As a chef, I have owned many kitchen gadgets over the years. More often than not, these magical contraptions were used a couple of times then hidden away in a cupboard. After many years and lots of unused equipment, I realized that a minimalist approach often leads to the best recipes. I now focus on fewer pieces of high-quality equipment that will last a lifetime—you'll need only a handful of essential tools to cook any recipe in this book. I have included what I consider to be two luxury items that I use almost daily—a high-speed blender (I have a Vitamix) and a dehydrator. I cannot recommend them enough—they will change your life in the kitchen and give you amazing results.

DEHYDRATOR

A dehydrator is a low-temperature oven about the size of a microwave, with four to nine sliding or stacked mesh trays that allow air to freely circulate. A dehydrator slowly removes the moisture from foods, making them dense and chewy (think breads, cookies, burgers, kale chips, and granola). You can also use it to control the fermentation of cheeses, yogurts, and veggies. A dehydrator cooks the ingredients while still maintaining their nutritional integrity.

In general, the recipes in this book are dehydrated at a temperature of 115°F. You should always consider dehydrating times approximate, as the temperature of your machine, the temperature of your kitchen, and humidity can all affect how long your foods will need to dehydrate. My best advice is to check the food frequently until you get to know your machine. Keeping the dehydrator on your counter will motivate you to make delicious recipes and simple fares like fruit leathers with ripe, seasonal fruit, cookies and crackers made from pulp, and your own creations that the techniques in this book will inspire. Dehydrators are very forgiving, and it's safe to leave them running 24/7. You can throw something in to test for fun and run off to work. Nothing will burn, and you can often "rehydrate" an overdried trial with water if need be.

One of my favorite things to do is to add something to the dehydrator at night right before bed and then wake up in the morning to something delicious already prepared for breakfast!

NONSTICK BAKING SHEETS

You will need flexible silicone baking sheets to use with your dehydrator. As a "baking" surface, you can use them to line your trays for making fruit leathers, crackers, and pizza crusts. They will give you the ease and freedom to make large batches of a recipe or single ingredients, allowing you to reshape and flip your ingredients after you transfer them from the bowl or blender. These sheets can be washed and reused for years.

FOOD PROCESSOR

I've had my food processor for over ten years, and it still works like a dream. A good food processor has a heavy, strong motor that will not give up. They usually come with several attachments that serve different purposes: The only blade I actually use is the S-shaped blade that sits in the bottom of the bowl and is used for grinding, mincing, and chopping. They also come with a shredding and a slicing blade, both of which are flat disks with holes or crescents respectively.

GLASS JARS

Mason jars, Weck jars, and recycled jars (leftover from coconut oil, nut butters, etc.) are indispensable for storing your dehydrated goods, soups, nut milks, salad dressings, sauces, and much more. They make really good fermenting jars too—just make sure to sterilize them with boiling water beforehand.

HIGH-SPEED BLENDER

It took me too many years to invest in one, and I can't say enough about mine. If you enjoy cooking, a high-speed blender can be life changing. This is definitely an investment, but it is indispensable for making everything from nut milks and smoothies to flours, ice cream, dressings, and soups. The more powerful your blender, the more air it can whip into ingredients—completely transforming them in a matter of minutes. For the ultimate in texture and speed, I believe a Vitamix is truly the best option, and although expensive, it will last a lifetime. That said, the recipes in this book can be made with a regular blender. Blending may just take a bit longer, and the end result won't be as silky smooth—but it will still be delicious!

JUICER

Juicing is a wonderful way to make nutrients readily absorbable. A good juicer will extract the most juice possible from your produce without oxidation, as well as the most nutrients and enzymes, drop for drop. If you have a hard time getting your daily fruits and veggies, this is a great alternative; drinking fresh juices is as close as you can get to eating raw, organic vegetables, herbs, and fruits without actually doing so. Drinking pressed juice is part of my daily ritual, and I love starting each day with so many nutrients. Fresh juices can be deeply calming to the nervous system, and all the vitamins can easily be absorbed into the body without taxing the digestive system.

A cold-press juicer extracts the juice from your produce very slowly, which allows the juice to retain more of the plant's nutrients and enzymes, without lots of oxidation. It works through pressure—squeezing the juice out of leaves, roots, vegetables, and fruit by crushing the cell walls. Due to the way it is extracted, cold-pressed juice has the longest shelf life (up to seventy-two hours in the refrigerator), so it can also be a time saver, letting you make

a big batch every three days instead of one every day. Although it's the most expensive type of juicer, it extracts much more juice from your produce and will save you money in the long run, especially if you drink juice daily.

MANDOLINE

The mandoline is an excellent tool for anyone who loves to cook with plants. It quickly slices vegetables and fruit into delicate, paper-thin slices that look beautiful. It's a great way to minimize your prep time and really adds that extra something to a dish, but you can use a knife to gain a similar effect if you don't own one. They are usually affordable, small, light, and super easy to clean and store. Some mandolines will slice, grate, and shave, with adjustable blades for different cutting styles and thicknesses.

NUT MILK BAG

These bags are made from fine-mesh cloth, and they are ideal for straining the pulp from nut milks. They make the separation of the nut from the liquid a breeze, resulting in a silky-smooth texture. These bags are perfect because they can be washed and reused. I like to keep washed and dried bags in the freezer in the interest of food safety. You can also use a clean cotton tea towel, which works beautifully.

ONE SHARP KNIFE

I own several knives that I take really good care of, but the truth is that I tend to use the one favorite knife in my collection: a big chef's knife that my hand knows well. It's essential that you sharpen your knife regularly so that it can do anything from cutting up a thick-skinned kabocha squash to slicing a juicy tomato. If you take good care of a good knife it will last a lifetime, but be sure to keep it well honed using a special whetstone, block, or honing steel. Don't put your knives in the dishwasher—always wash your knife gently and carefully with the tips of your fingers or a dishcloth and clean the blade on both sides using lukewarm water and a little soap. Dry it well before putting it away.

SPIRALIZER

The spiralizer is an absolutely amazing invention for making noodles from vegetables and fruit. It cuts hard vegetables and fruit into thin ribbons as delicate as angel hair pasta. I prefer standing models over handheld ones because they are efficient and they make it less likely you'll get cut.

STEAMER BASKET

A steamer basket is a handy tool for steaming vegetables. It can also double as a strainer on the sly. I like the steamers that come in a set with a matching pot. Steaming vegetables is a simple solution for breaking down tough cellulose to aid in digestion, making the nutrients easier absorbed and more efficient. Lightly steaming certain vegetables makes them more tender and tasty with minimal harm done to their precious enzymes and nutrients.

VEGETABLE BRUSH

This is a must for veggie lovers, especially if you consume organic root vegetables like carrots or beets, which you will want to eat unpeeled for their full nutritional value. These brushes have the sole and simple purpose of cleaning dirt off the vegetable while retaining all but the thinnest outer layer of nutrient-rich skin.

PART THREE

RADIANT RECIPES

DRINKS

I just love drinks. Juices, smoothies, nut and seed milks, teas, and tonics are some of the easiest ways to get a powerful dose of beauty nutrients. Drinks can transform nuts, seeds, vegetables, fruits, and herbs into medicinal nectars capable of healing the body and mind and helping skin look refreshed, hydrated, and healthier than ever before. They can be the most nutrient-dense fuel around—loaded with proteins, enzymes, vitamins, trace minerals, and other vital elements. You will notice that some recipes have an option called "Beauty Add-Ins"—these can be herbs, adaptogens, or spices that are natural beauty enhancers. They are by no means compulsory but are rather meant to serve as inspirational guides if you want to start playing with these ingredients to complement a recipe.

FOUNTAIN OF YOUTH

I drink this refreshing juice nearly every day during warmer months because it is so hydrating—the cucumber and pineapple have a high water content and really help to lock moisture into your skin cells. I just love the sweetness of the pineapple and the punchy overtones of the cilantro. Cilantro is a powerhouse plant with antioxidants that help prevent wrinkles, sagging skin, and pigmentation. It is also rich in linoleic acid (also known as vitamin F)—a known problem-solver for blackheads and great at hydrating skin and hair.

1 BIG GLASS
OR 2 SMALL ONES

Juicer

½ pineapple, skin removed

1 cucumber

1 cup firmly packed kale, or to taste

½ lemon, peeled

4 sprigs of fresh cilantro, or to taste

Coarsely chop all the ingredients and process through the juicer, alternating among the veggies and fruits. Stir and serve.

SUN SEEKER

This delicious juice is another favorite of mine for summer days. When I was young, my grandmother used carrot juice on her face to protect it from sun damage. It seemed strange at the time, but as it turns out, carrots are rich in carotenoids—the antioxidants that reduce the negative effects of ultraviolet rays. This pigment is actually used as sunscreen by plants and can activate the melanin in your skin.

Although I wouldn't use this juice in place of sunscreen, it can provide extra protection from the sun's effects, from the inside out.

1 BIG GLASS
OR 2 SMALL ONES

Juicer

3 carrots

1 apple

½-inch piece of fresh ginger

¼-inch piece of fresh turmeric

Coarsely chop all the ingredients and process through the juicer, alternating among the veggies and fruit. Stir and serve.

COLLAGEN BOOST

Collagen is the main protein in our skin, and it is largely responsible for keeping it plump and youthful, combating wrinkles, sagging skin, and cellulite. The good news is that you can get more collagen by consuming vitamin C–rich foods such as strawberries, oranges, and pineapple. This juice will help keep your skin glowing and bright while supporting its underlying structure.

I BIG GLASS
OR 2 SMALL ONES

Juicer

½ pineapple, skin removed

2 oranges, peeled and separated into segments

1 cup strawberries

Coarsely chop the pineapple, then process all the ingredients through the juicer, alternating among the fruits. Stir and serve.

BRIGHT EYES

The best-known nutrient in carrots (and other orange plants) is of course beta-carotene—the powerful antioxidant that gives these fruits and vegetables their brilliant color. Beta-carotene also helps to make vitamin A, which promotes eye health and helps protect your skin from sun damage.

I BIG GLASS
OR 2 SMALL ONES

Juicer

3 carrots

½ pineapple, skin removed

½-inch (or larger) piece of fresh turmeric

Coarsely chop all the ingredients and process through the juicer, alternating among the veggies and fruit. Stir and serve.

A BREATH OF FRESH AIR

We all have heard how important it is to be aware of our breath. This juice is inspired by a ten-day challenge I participated in. I committed to focusing on consciously breathing for 10 to 30 minutes a day. I couldn't believe the difference just breathing made in my overall productivity *and* the smoothness of my skin—I could feel the soft suppleness every time I touched my face. This juice has beets as the active ingredient, which are rich in beneficial nitrites (the good kind!) that help open up your blood vessels for more oxygen flow and lower blood pressure.

I BIG GLASS
OR 2 SMALL ONES

Juicer

3 carrots

½ pineapple, skin removed

1 beet

Handful of kale

Small handful of chard

½ cup blueberries

½ lemon, peeled

Coarsely chop all the ingredients except the blueberries. Process all the ingredients through the juicer, alternating among the veggies and fruits. Stir and serve.

NATURAL BEAUTY

Why not kick-start your day with a hydrating, wrinkle-preventing berry smoothie? This drink is bubbling with detoxifying antioxidants and packed with collagen-forming vitamin C. The good fats in the coconut milk will help with maximum absorption of these nutrients, and the acai makes it the ultimate skin tonic for an overall glow.

MAKES 2 CUPS

2 cups unsweetened coconut milk or plant milk of choice

1 frozen banana

4 Medjool dates, pitted

¼ cup fresh or frozen blueberries

¼ cup fresh or frozen strawberries

¼ cup fresh or frozen raspberries

Zest and juice of 1 lime

2 teaspoons acai powder

1 teaspoon chia seeds

¼ teaspoon vanilla bean powder

Combine all the ingredients in a blender and blend on high speed until smooth and creamy. Pour into a glass and serve.

Alluring Matcha

Natural Beauty (p. 73)

ALLURING MATCHA

Crazy about matcha? I love this energetic potion that delivers stamina without the crash. Matcha boosts both your metabolism and your creativity, and—an added bonus—it is incredibly cleansing. The chlorophyll adds to matcha's effectiveness, as it cleanses the blood and acts as an excellent detoxifier.

I drink this potion every time I need to focus on my work and feel inspired, and it always does the trick. Matcha enhances concentration, and the polyphenols and catechins present in matcha promote simultaneous relaxation, something that coffee can't brag. Perfectly balanced with spice and sweetness, this smoothie is impossible to resist!

MAKES 2 CUPS

2 cups unsweetened coconut milk or plant milk of choice

2 teaspoons raw honey or sweetener of choice

2 teaspoons fresh ginger juice

½ teaspoon matcha

½ teaspoon ground cardamom

½ teaspoon liquid or powder chlorophyll

¼ teaspoon vanilla bean powder

Pinch of ground cinnamon

BEAUTY ADD-INS (OPTIONAL)

1 teaspoon lucuma powder

¼ teaspoon pearl powder

Combine all the ingredients in a blender and blend on high speed until smooth. Serve cold or warmed.

BROWNIE MACA

You can energize both body and mind naturally with the powerful combination of cacao and maca. This smoothie, which tastes like a gooey caramel brownie, will give you a boost of energy and clarity to prepare you for a day full of activities and creativity.

MAKES 2 CUPS

2 cups unsweetened coconut milk or plant milk of choice

1 frozen banana

2 to 4 Medjool dates, pitted

2 tablespoons cacao powder

2 tablespoons maca powder

1 tablespoon almond butter

1 tablespoon hemp seeds

¼ teaspoon ground cinnamon

¼ teaspoon vanilla bean powder

Combine all the ingredients in a blender and blend on high speed until smooth and creamy. Pour into a glass and serve.

Brownie Maca

The Detox (p. 80)

Invincible Coffee (p. 78)

INVINCIBLE COFFEE

This is my version of "keto coffee." I make it with spiced cold-pressed coffee, which has lower acidity than hot-brewed coffee, and is easier to digest for those sensitive to acidic foods. Healthy fats in the coconut oil and ghee provide brain power, mental clarity, and energy, and support hormonal balance. The cacao is a natural aphrodisiac and mojo booster, and it also is one of the highest natural sources of magnesium, which helps with detoxification, including of the skin, as well as being essential for healthy bones and teeth.

MAKES 2 CUPS

1 cup Spiced Cold Brew (recipe follows)

1 cup unsweetened coconut milk or plant milk of choice

1 tablespoon cacao powder

2 teaspoons coconut sugar or sweetener of choice

1 tablespoon ghee or coconut oil

1 teaspoon mesquite powder

BEAUTY ADD-INS (OPTIONAL)

¼ teaspoon pearl powder

Combine the spiced cold brew with the coconut milk, cacao powder, coconut sugar, ghee, mesquite powder, and pearl powder, if using, in a blender and blend on high speed until smooth. Serve cold or warmed.

SPICED COLD BREW

MAKES 8 CUPS

1 cup freshly ground coffee

1 tablespoon plus 1 teaspoon ground cardamom

2 teaspoons dried rose petals

2 teaspoons ground cinnamon

1 teaspoon freshly grated nutmeg

8 cups water, unheated

Put the coffee, cardamom, rose petals, cinnamon, and nutmeg in a big glass jar. Pour in the water and stir gently until well combined. Cover with a lid and let steep for 18 to 24 hours, either at room temperature or in the refrigerator.

Strain the coffee mixture through a fine-mesh sieve set over a large bowl to remove the larger grounds. Discard the grounds. Clean the sieve, place it on the jar, and line with a coffee filter, nut milk bag, or a few sheets of paper towel. Strain the coffee back into the jar. Strain the coffee back and forth between the bowl and jar two or three times, until no murky residue is left. Stored in a sealed glass jar in the refrigerator, this spiced cold brew will keep for 1 month or so.

THE DETOX

Charcoal, a powerful detoxifier and purifier, is showing up in everything from smoothies to toothpaste. Charcoal has little to no taste, so it can easily be added to drinks without any unpleasant aftertaste. This magical drink removes toxins, improves digestion, reduces bloating, and prevents cell damage. Have it once a week or every month, especially after you overindulge or eat less-healthy foods.

MAKES 2 CUPS

2 cups coconut water

1 cup frozen pineapple chunks

1 teaspoon activated charcoal powder

Leaves from 1 sprig of fresh mint

Tip: You can also purchase activated charcoal made from coconut shells—just be sure you pick a brand that does not include sorbitol, which can lead to intestinal distress and adverse side effects.

Combine all the ingredients in a blender and blend on high speed until smooth. Pour into a glass and serve.

INFUSED FLORAL MILK

These supercharged infused milks will make a perfect part of your daily regimen for firmer skin, stronger hair, and a more even complexion. This powerful, creamy infused potion extracts every last vitamin, mineral, and antioxidant that the leaves and flowers have to offer. And above all else, the nutrients in these milks are bioavailable, rapidly absorbed by the body, so their positive effects are felt more quickly—you can literally feel the mineralization within moments. You will need to get the nuts soaking and the flowers steeping the night before you plan to make it.

MAKES 4 CUPS

1 cup nuts of choice (such as almonds, cashews, or macadamia nuts)

2 tablespoons dried rose petals or chamomile flowers, or 1 tablespoon dried lavender flowers

2 teaspoons raw honey

¼ teaspoon vanilla bean powder

Pinch of pink salt

BEAUTY ADD-INS (OPTIONAL)

½ teaspoon pearl powder

½ teaspoon schisandra powder

Put the nuts into a jug or bowl, cover with plenty of water, and place in the refrigerator. Put the flowers in a 1-quart glass jar and fill the jar to the top with filtered water. Cover the jar and place in the fridge or leave on the countertop. Let the nuts soak and the flowers steep overnight.

Strain the floral water through a fine-mesh sieve placed over a blender. Drain the nuts and add to the blender. Add the honey, vanilla powder, and pink salt. Add the pearl and schisandra powders, if using, and blend on high speed until smooth. Strain through a nut milk bag or fine-mesh sieve and serve.

AWAKEN BEAUTY MILK

The best thing that ever happened to your caffeine-craving self, this creamy coffee nut milk is the ultimate cold, caffeinated treat. Fats from the macadamia nuts keep the caffeine from hitting your bloodstream too quickly and the fresh vanilla bean rounds things out for the perfect flavor.

MAKES 4 CUPS

1 cup macadamia nuts, soaked (see page 50)

4 cups Spiced Cold Brew (page 70)

2 teaspoons raw honey

Pinch of pink salt

2 Medjool dates, pitted

2 tablespoons cacao powder

2 tablespoons maca powder

2 teaspoons lucuma powder

¼ teaspoon vanilla bean powder

BEAUTY ADD-INS (OPTIONAL)

¼ teaspoon pearl powder

¼ teaspoon cordyceps powder

Put the macadamia nuts into a jug or bowl and cover with plenty of water. Let soak overnight in the refrigerator.

Drain the nuts and transfer to a blender. Add 4 cups of water and the honey and salt. Blend on high speed until smooth. Strain through a nut milk bag or fine-mesh sieve placed over a bowl. Discard the pulp or, to save it for another use, store in a sealed container in the fridge.

Return the macadamia milk to the blender and add the dates, the cacao, maca, and lucuma powders, and the vanilla powder. Add the pearl and cordyceps powders, if using, and blend on high speed until smooth.

THE BIG BLUE

This alluring blue beauty milk gets its color from mineral-rich blue-green algae. Its name was inspired by one of my favorite movies, *The Big Blue*, because its gorgeous color reminds me of all those amazing deep-water dives, the dolphins, and how much I love the sea. Algae is packed with powerful nutrients (over sixty-five of them) and antioxidants, and it is an inflammation tamer too.

MAKES 2 CUPS

2 cups coconut water

¼ cup fresh coconut meat

¼ teaspoon blue-green algae

¼ teaspoon vanilla bean powder

Sweetener of choice (optional)

BEAUTY ADD-INS (OPTIONAL)

1 teaspoon lucuma powder

½ teaspoon he shou wu powder

Combine all the ingredients in a blender and blend on high speed until smooth. Add sweetener to taste, if desired.

SALTED CARAMEL MILK

With such a luscious combination of ingredients, this drink tastes a little too delicious to be healthy (but I promise it is!). A dollop of tahini gives it depth of flavor as well as essential beauty nutrients such as copper, manganese, calcium, magnesium, phosphorus, iron, and zinc, which will leave your skin, hair, and nails strong and glowing.

MAKES 2 CUPS

1½ cups unsweetened almond milk or plant milk of choice

½ cup Spiced Cold Brew (page 79)

4 Medjool dates, pitted

1 tablespoon tahini

1 teaspoon maca powder

1 teaspoon mesquite powder

1 teaspoon lucuma powder

Pinch of pink salt

Sweetener of choice (optional)

Combine all the ingredients in a blender and blend on high speed until smooth. Add sweetener to taste, if desired.

SEAFOAM LATTE

This is a truly whimsical latte, made of the most nutrient-dense superfood, blue-green algae, a powerhouse of protein and antioxidants that will support your health and beauty. This warming concoction has a mildly spicy taste due to the ginger, which boosts immunity and aids in detoxification.

MAKES 2 CUPS

2 cups unsweetened coconut milk or plant milk of choice

2 teaspoons raw honey or sweetener of choice

1 teaspoon ghee or coconut oil

1 teaspoon ground ginger, or 1 tablespoon grated fresh ginger

¼ teaspoon blue-green algae

Pinch of vanilla bean powder

Pinch of beet powder (optional)

BEAUTY ADD-INS (OPTIONAL)

½ teaspoon reishi powder

¼ teaspoon pearl powder

Gently warm the coconut milk in a small saucepan over low heat, without allowing it to simmer. Carefully pour it into a blender. Add the honey, ghee, ginger, blue-green algae, and vanilla powder. Add the reishi and pearl powders, if using. Blend on high speed until warm and frothy. Pour into a mug and sprinkle with a little beet powder, if desired.

DETOX LATTE

This ultra-detoxifying latte is an internal sweeper, getting hold of toxins and helping to flush them out. Don't be put off by the color: charcoal is quite taste free.

MAKES 2 CUPS

2 cups unsweetened coconut milk or plant milk of choice

1 tablespoon mesquite powder

2 teaspoons lucuma powder

1 teaspoon maca powder

2 teaspoons raw honey or sweetener of choice

1 teaspoon ghee or coconut oil

¼ teaspoon activated charcoal

¼ teaspoon vanilla bean powder

Gently warm the coconut milk in a small saucepan over low heat, without allowing it to simmer. Carefully pour it into a blender. Add the mesquite, lucuma and maca powders, honey, ghee, charcoal, and vanilla powder, and blend on high speed until warm and frothy. Pour into a mug and serve.

ROSE QUARTZ LATTE

Widely used in Ayurveda to tame inflammation and calm the body and mind, and an eternal symbol of true love and beauty, rose is a soothing antidote to the physical stresses of everyday living. Rose water and petals support the liver in its never-ending quest to facilitate detoxification, and they serve as a gentle diuretic, promoting healthy and regular elimination. Rose also acts as a blood purifier, helping to remove and neutralize toxins. Much like rose quartz, this delicate and soothing latte is purifying and opens the heart chakra, bringing about calming and peaceful frequencies.

MAKES 2 CUPS

2 cups unsweetened coconut milk or plant milk of choice

2 tablespoons fresh beet juice

1 teaspoon rose water

1 teaspoon cacao butter or ghee, melted

1 teaspoon raw honey or sweetener of choice

¼ teaspoon vanilla bean powder

Rose petals, for garnish (optional)

BEAUTY ADD-INS (OPTIONAL)

½ teaspoon schisandra powder

¼ teaspoon pearl powder

Gently warm the coconut milk and beet juice in a small saucepan over low heat, without allowing it to simmer. Carefully pour it into a blender. Add the rose water, cacao butter, honey, and vanilla powder. Add the schisandra and pearl powders, if using, and blend on high speed until warm and frothy. Pour into a mug and sprinkle with rose petals, if desired.

CARROT CAKE LATTE

The sweet, earthy carrots, creamy coconut milk, and warming spices in this delicious drink support your immune system and boost energy while promoting a beautiful radiant glow. I love to drink this in the morning to start off my day with a sure hit of immune-boosting vitamin C and skin-plumping beta-carotene.

MAKES 2 CUPS

1 cup fresh carrot juice

1 cup unsweetened coconut milk or plant milk of choice

4 Medjool dates

1 tablespoon coconut butter

1 teaspoon lucuma powder

½ teaspoon ground ginger

¼ teaspoon ground turmeric

¼ teaspoon freshly grated nutmeg, plus more for optional garnish

Pinch of vanilla bean powder

Pinch of freshly ground black pepper

BEAUTY ADD-INS (OPTIONAL)

½ teaspoon ashwagandha powder

Gently warm the carrot juice and coconut milk in a small saucepan over low heat, without allowing it to simmer. Carefully pour it into a blender. Add the dates, coconut butter, lucuma powder, ginger, turmeric, nutmeg, vanilla powder, and black pepper. Blend on high speed until warm and frothy. Pour into a mug and sprinkle with a little more nutmeg, if desired.

CH. 2

BREAKFAST

These beautifying breakfast recipes are meant to be drool-worthy enough to get you out of bed and so delicious you can't wait for tomorrow morning to come. Whether you have zero time to kill between waking and work time or are planning a full spread for a weekend brunch, there's something healthy, filling, pretty, and sweet here for everyone.

ACAI CACAO BOWL

Take your power-breakfast game to the next level with this acai bowl—chock full of beauty nutrients and age-defying antioxidants that are great for energy and luminous skin. This recipe is inspired by my favorite acai spot in Kauai, where they always drizzle a generous amount of peanut butter on top! This versatile bowl has so many options for superfood toppings, it is easy to change them up when the moods strikes.

SERVES 2

4 acai frozen packs (3.5 ounces each), or 2 cups frozen acai berries

2 frozen bananas

¼ cup unsweetened coconut milk or plant milk of choice, plus more if needed

3 tablespoons cacao powder

TOPPINGS

1 sliced banana

¼ cup Tropical Matcha Granola (page 108)

2 tablespoons dried goji berries

2 tablespoons crushed macadamia nuts

2 tablespoons cacao nibs

2 tablespoons unsweetened coconut chips

Pinch of ground cinnamon

Good drizzle of unsalted peanut butter

Good drizzle of Chocolate Coating (page 254)

Combine the frozen acai, frozen bananas, coconut milk, and cacao powder in a high-speed blender and blend until thick and creamy. Add more coconut milk if needed to achieve the desired consistency. Divide between two bowls and decorate with the toppings.

GLOW BOWL

This breakfast bowl is pure indulgence—the combination of the creamy caramel with the subtle depth of the tahini is amazing. Tahini is a paste made from ground sesame seeds, it contains just about every type of vitamin B your body needs, helping to bolster your nervous system and your overall immunity. It's also full of iron, which helps to improve skin tone, and vitamin E, which helps skin retain moisture, keeping it smooth and silky.

SERVES 2

2 cups frozen bananas

1 cup fresh or frozen coconut meat

1 cup Spiced Cold Brew (page 79)

4 large Medjool dates, pitted

2 tablespoons tahini

1 tablespoon lucuma powder

1 tablespoon mesquite powder

1 tablespoon maca powder

1 teaspoon ground cardamom

1 teaspoon reishi powder

TOPPINGS

¼ cup Tropical Matcha Granola (page 108)

1 sliced banana

2 tablespoons unsweetened coconut chips

Combine all the ingredients in a high-speed blender and blend until thick and creamy. Divide between two bowls and decorate with the toppings.

MERMAID BOWL

This refreshing, colorful bowl is ridiculously gorgeous as well as delicious. With the sweetness of tropical fruit, the energy and zen of matcha, and the powerful nutrients of blue-green algae, this vibrant bowl will change your mornings forever.

SERVES 2

2 frozen bananas

1 cup frozen mango

1 cup fresh coconut meat

Zest and juice of ½ lime

2 teaspoons fresh ginger juice

½ teaspoon matcha

¼ teaspoon blue-green algae or spirulina

1½ cups coconut water, plus more if needed

TOPPINGS

¼ cup Tropical Matcha Granola (page 108)

2 tablespoons unsweetened coconut chips

2 tablespoons white mulberries

2 tablespoons hemp seeds

Combine all the ingredients in a high-speed blender and blend until thick and creamy. Add more coconut water if needed to achieve the desired consistency. Divide between two bowls and decorate with toppings, if using.

GLOWING SKIN BIRCHER

This classic Australian breakfast is traditionally made with oats, but my version is heavy on chia seeds for skin regeneration and spiked with acai to brighten complexion and the free radicals that cause premature aging. It is super easy to put together the night before and have all ready for breakfast the next morning.

SERVES 2

¼ cup chia seeds

2 tablespoons gluten-free oats

1 tablespoon acai powder

1 teaspoon vanilla bean powder

1 teaspoon lime zest

Pinch of ground ginger

2 cups unsweetened coconut milk or plant milk of choice

2 tablespoons coconut nectar or sweetener of choice

TOPPINGS

½ apple, grated

2 tablespoons berries of choice

2 tablespoons hemp seeds

2 tablespoons cacao nibs

Put the chia seeds, oats, acai powder, vanilla powder, lime zest, and ginger into a 1-quart glass jar with a tight-fitting lid. Cover and shake to combine. Add the coconut milk and coconut nectar, re-cover, and shake vigorously for 3 minutes. Transfer to the refrigerator to chill for 30 to 45 minutes, until the mixture has a pudding-like consistency, shaking every 10 minutes so that it doesn't clump together.

Divide the pudding between two bowls, add toppings, if using, and enjoy immediately, or store the pudding in the refrigerator for up to 5 days.

ZEN CHIA PUDDING
WITH MATCHA WHIP

These glowy matcha cups are jam-packed with amazing nutrition. Chia seeds are high in omega-3s and quality fiber, and the matcha offers concentrated antioxidants and other complexion-boosting nutrients. This superfood breakfast will fill you up, keep you both hydrated and regular, and provide your system with deep nourishment. It also makes a delicious dessert!

SERVES 4

PUDDING

4 cups unsweetened coconut milk or plant milk of choice

2 tablespoons plus 1½ teaspoons coconut nectar or sweetener of choice

1 teaspoon matcha

½ teaspoon vanilla bean powder

¾ cup chia seeds

MATCHA WHIP

1 cup young Thai coconut meat

¼ to ½ cup coconut water

1 teaspoon matcha

½ teaspoon vanilla bean powder

1 tablespoon coconut nectar or sweetener of choice

BEAUTY ADD-INS (OPTIONAL)

1 teaspoon lucuma powder

¼ teaspoon pearl powder

TOPPINGS

Berries or chopped fresh fruit of choice

To make the pudding, put the coconut milk, coconut nectar, matcha, vanilla powder, and any beauty add-ins you'd like into a half-gallon jar with a tight-fitting lid. Cover and shake to combine. Add the chia seeds and shake vigorously for a couple of minutes so the chia doesn't clump together. Transfer to the refrigerator to chill for about 1 hour, until the mixture has a thick pudding-like consistency.

In the meantime, to make the matcha whip, combine all the ingredients in a high-speed blender and blend until smooth. Transfer to a glass jar with a tight-fitting lid. Cover and transfer to the fridge to chill for about 1 hour, until set.

To serve, spoon the chia pudding into bowls and top with the matcha cream and seasonal fruit. Stored separately in the fridge, the pudding will keep for up to 5 days, and the cream will keep for up to 4 days.

TROPICAL MATCHA GRANOLA

This antiaging, energy-enhancing, memory-boosting granola is everything you need to start your morning right. It's antioxidant packed, totally addictive, and detox-friendly, so you can snack on it as much as you like. Eat with milk, sprinkle over coconut milk yogurt with fruit, or munch it by the handful.

MAKES 9 CUPS

Dehydrator

3 cups buckwheat groats, soaked

2 cups sliced fresh pineapple and/or papaya

1 cup mulberries

1 cup golden flaxseeds

1 cup unsweetened coconut chips

½ cup chopped crystallized ginger

1 tablespoon matcha

1 tablespoon orange zest

1 tablespoon lime zest

2 teaspoons vanilla bean powder

Generous pinch of pink salt

1 cup fresh orange juice

⅓ cup macadamia nut butter or raw nut butter of choice

¼ cup maple syrup or sweetener of choice

2 tablespoons freshly squeezed lime juice

Line 2 dehydrator trays with nonstick baking sheets.

Put the buckwheat groats, pineapple and/or papaya, mulberries, flaxseeds, coconut chips, ginger, matcha, orange zest, lime zest, vanilla powder, and salt in a large bowl and stir to combine. Combine the orange juice, macadamia butter, maple syrup, and lime juice in a blender and blend on high speed until smooth. Pour over the dry mixture and stir until well combined.

Spread the mixture evenly over the prepared dehydrator trays and place in the dehydrator. Dehydrate for 10 hours (see page 59). Using a spatula, flip the granola over, then break the granola into small pieces and dehydrate for another 6 hours, or until dry. Let cool.

Transfer the cooled granola to an airtight container and store at room temperature for up to 2 months.

ACAI BEAUTY BARS

What's better than a batch of healthy, beautifying breakfast bars? A batch of bars you don't have to bake. These no-bake breakfast bars are packed with antioxidants, fiber, good fats, and protein. Perfectly portable and the perfect make-ahead breakfast (or snack), you can make them on the weekend and keep them in the refrigerator for the whole week. The ingredients are super flexible too, so feel free to change up the flavors and ingredients depending on what you have on hand.

MAKES 8

BASE

1 cup nuts (such as almonds, cashews, or macadamias; see page 50), soaked

1 cup sunflower seeds

1 cup Medjool dates, pitted

½ cup cacao powder

¼ cup unsweetened coconut chips

¼ cup cacao nibs

3 tablespoons hemp seeds

2 tablespoons flaxseeds

2 tablespoons maca powder

2 tablespoons almond butter or tahini

2 tablespoons coconut nectar or sweetener of choice

1 tablespoon lucuma powder

FILLING

1 cup fresh or frozen raspberries

½ cup cashews, soaked (see page 50)

½ cup chia seeds

2 tablespoons acai powder

2 tablespoons coconut nectar or sweetener of choice

2 tablespoons coconut butter

1 tablespoon coconut oil

1 tablespoon almond butter

1 teaspoon vanilla bean powder

TOPPINGS

2 tablespoons hemp seeds

2 tablespoons unsweetened coconut chips

2 tablespoons cacao nibs

Line a baking pan with parchment paper and set aside.

To make the base, pulse the nuts in a food processor to break them up a bit. Add the sunflower seeds, dates, cacao powder, coconut chips, cacao nibs, hemp seeds, flaxseeds, maca powder, almond butter, coconut nectar, and lucuma powder, and process until just combined (be careful not to overblend). Transfer the mixture into the prepared pan and distribute evenly, then press firmly into the bottom of the pan. Refrigerate while you prepare the filling.

To make the filling, combine all the ingredients in a blender and blend on high speed until smooth and creamy. Pour the filling over the chilled base and spread evenly with a rubber spatula. Sprinkle liberally with the toppings. Refrigerate for 2 hours, or until set, then cut into bars.

Bars will keep for 4 days in the refrigerator or up to 3 months in the freezer.

CACAO CREPES
WITH RAW HAZELNUT BUTTER & COCONUT WHIPPED CREAM

Some weekends were made for breakfast in bed, and these chocolaty beauties are just what you need to add a little flair to your Saturday morning routine. These gluten-free crepes are as mouth-watering as they look and, as far as sweet breakfasts go, deliciously guilt-free: they are made mainly out of bananas, for skin elasticity and natural radiance, and flaxseeds, which give them a dose of omega-3 for soft, clear skin. If you want to impress someone, this should do the trick.

SERVES 4

Dehydrator

CREPES

4 medium bananas, peeled and chopped

2 tablespoons flax meal

1 tablespoon freshly squeezed lime juice

2 teaspoons ground cinnamon

1 teaspoon vanilla bean powder

Pinch of pink salt

TO SERVE

Raw Hazelnut Butter
(recipe follows)

Coconut Whipped Cream
(recipe follows)

Line two dehydrator trays with nonstick baking sheets.

To make the crepes, combine all the ingredients in a blender and blend on high speed until smooth. Scoop ¼ cup the batter onto a prepared dehydrator tray and, using a rubber spatula or the back of a spoon, spread the crepe thinly and evenly into a circle. Repeat the process with the rest of the batter. Load the dehydrator with the trays and dehydrate for 8 hours, or until set but still pliable (see page 59). Serve immediately with a dollop of hazelnut spread and whipped cream on top of each crepe, or wrap up in pieces of parchment paper for up to 1 week in the refrigerator or up to 2 months in the freezers.

RAW HAZELNUT BUTTER

MAKES 2 CUPS

1 cup hazelnut butter or raw nut butter of choice (cashew also works really well), at room temperature

¼ cup coconut sugar or sweetener of choice

2 tablespoons cacao powder

2 tablespoons cacao butter, melted

½ teaspoon vanilla bean powder

Pinch of pink salt

BEAUTY ADD-IN (OPTIONAL)

1 teaspoon chaga powder

Put all the ingredients into a small bowl and whisk until smooth and creamy. Store in an airtight jar in the refrigerator for up to a month.

COCONUT WHIPPED CREAM

MAKES 2 CUPS

1½ cups young Thai coconut meat

¼ to ½ cup coconut water

1 teaspoon vanilla bean powder

Combine all the ingredients in a high-speed blender and blend until smooth and creamy. Transfer to a glass jar, cover with a lid, and chill in the refrigerator for 1 hour to set before serving. This cream will keep in its jar in the fridge for 3 days.

PORTOBELLO BENEDICT
WITH CASHEW HOLLANDAISE

This modern twist on a classic Benedict might be one of my favorite breakfasts. Unlike traditional eggs Benedict, this version is loaded with ingredients that are nourishing as well as delicious. Avocado and a cashew turmeric hollandaise give you that dose of beneficial fats to help speed up your metabolism, sharpen your concentration, balance your hormones, and illuminate your skin. You can make the hollandaise up to 5 days ahead.

SERVES 4

Dehydrator

WILTED SPINACH

4 cups baby spinach

1 tablespoon extra-virgin olive oil

1 tablespoon freshly squeezed lemon juice

Pink salt

Freshly ground black pepper

MUSHROOM BASES

2 to 3 tablespoons extra-virgin olive oil

2 teaspoons tamari

1 teaspoon fresh thyme leaves

1 garlic clove, minced

8 portobello mushrooms, caps only

Pink salt

HOLLANDAISE

2 cups cashews, soaked (see page 50)

1 cup water

1 garlic clove

2 tablespoons freshly squeezed lemon juice

1 tablespoon nutritional yeast

1 teaspoon mustard of choice

1 scant teaspoon turmeric powder

1 teaspoon pink salt

TO SERVE

1 avocado, mashed

1 tablespoon sesame seeds, for garnish

½ teaspoon curry powder, for garnish

To wilt the spinach, put the spinach, olive oil, and lemon juice into a medium bowl and massage thoroughly with your hands until the leaves are evenly coated. Season with salt and black pepper to taste. Set aside.

To prepare the mushroom bases, first line your dehydrator trays with nonstick baking sheets. Whisk together the olive oil, tamari, thyme, and garlic in a large bowl. Add the mushrooms and turn to coat with the marinade. Place on the prepared dehydrator trays, sprinkle with salt, and dehydrate for 5 hours, or until tender (see page 59).

To make the hollandaise, combine all the ingredients in a high-speed blender and blend until very smooth and creamy. Store in a jar in the refrigerator for up to 5 days, if desired.

To serve, divide the wilted spinach among four plates. Top each pile of spinach with two warm portobello mushrooms, followed by a quarter of the mashed avocado (form into a perfectly rounded mound with a spoon or use a cookie scoop). Drizzle with the hollandaise sauce, sprinkle with the sesame seeds and a dust of curry powder, and serve.

117

SOUPS & SALADS

Bowl trends may come and go, but soups and salads will never go out of style. With the right ingredients, they can keep you nourished from the inside out and boost your metabolism to help you cleanse and detox your body. So choose your ingredients wisely!

CHILLED CUCUMBER SOUP

A summer staple, this deliciously hydrating soup is incredibly easy and quick to make. Cucumber is extremely cooling and perfect for hot summer. It is also high in vitamins C and K as well as silica, which makes this soup a perfect skin tonic when you need a little brightening.

SERVES 4

½ bunch of fresh chives

½ bunch of fresh parsley

4 cucumbers

2 avocados, cut into large dice, plus more for garnish

Juice of 2 lemons

½ cup unsweetened almond milk or water

2 tablespoons tahini

2 tablespoons pine nuts

1 tablespoon raw honey or sweetener of choice

½ shallot

Pink salt

Freshly ground black pepper

Chop a few sprigs each of fresh chives and parsley and set aside. Combine the remaining chives and parsley and the cucumbers, avocados, lemon juice, almond milk, tahini, pine nuts, honey, and shallot in a blender and blend on high speed until smooth. Add salt and black pepper to taste. To serve, ladle the soup into bowls and top with the extra cubed avocado and the chopped herbs.

DETOXING BEET SOUP

Avocado and ginger are great additions to this version of borscht. Plus, they have the added benefits of being super rich in antioxidants like glutathione, which detoxifies and cleanses the liver and stimulates its cell function. Eating this soup will boost energy, tame inflammation, and feed your immune system.

SERVES 4

SOUP

4 cups fresh orange juice

2 beets, grated

2 carrots, grated

2 red bell peppers, chopped

2 celery stalks, chopped

1 avocado

1 tablespoon minced fresh ginger

2 garlic cloves

2 tablespoons extra-virgin olive oil

2 tablespoons apple cider vinegar

2 tablespoons minced fresh cilantro

Pinch of cayenne (optional)

Pink salt

Freshly ground black pepper

GARNISHES

½ cup sprouted beans or seeds of choice (see page 31)

¼ cup chopped walnuts

¼ cup chopped fresh cilantro

To make the soup, combine all the ingredients in a blender and blend on high speed until smooth and creamy. If the mixture is too thick, dilute it with a little water. Season with salt and black pepper to taste. To serve, ladle the soup into bowls and garnish with the sprouts, walnuts, and cilantro.

TOM KA SOUP
WITH MUSHROOM PEARLS

When I was pregnant with my eldest daughter, I craved this Thai soup all the time. Its spicy coconut broth was so soothing that I ate it nearly every day. It has a delicious mix of energizing flavors such as ginger and lemongrass and the wonderful skin renewal properties of mushrooms and sprouts. A little hint of turmeric to aid in repairing DNA and taming inflammation doesn't hurt either.

SERVES 2

MUSHROOM PEARLS

2 cups shiitake mushrooms, sliced

¼ cup tamari

1 tablespoon toasted sesame oil

SOUP

4 cups coconut cream

2 lemongrass stalks, tender yellow parts only, roughly chopped

1-inch piece of galangal root or fresh ginger

2 Medjool dates, pitted

1 garlic clove, crushed

1 tablespoon Thai curry paste

½ teaspoon ground turmeric

2 tablespoons tamari

2 tablespoons extra-virgin olive oil, or 1 tablespoon coconut oil

Juice of 1 lime

¼ cup chopped fresh cilantro, plus extra whole leaves to serve

Pink salt

2 cups sprouted beans or seeds of choice (see page 31)

1 lime, cut into 4 wedges

Start by marinating the mushrooms: Whisk together the tamari and toasted sesame oil in a large bowl. Add the mushrooms and toss gently to cover them with the marinade. Set aside.

To make the soup, combine the coconut cream, lemongrass, galangal root, dates, garlic, curry paste, and turmeric in a blender and blend on high speed until smooth. Strain through a mesh sieve set over a bowl, then return the strained mixture to the blender. Add the tamari, olive oil, lime juice, and cilantro and pulse just to combine. Season with salt to taste.

To serve, divide the sprouts between bowls and pour the soup over. Decorate with the marinated mushrooms and cilantro leaves. Serve accompanied by lime wedges.

CREAMY ROASTED TOMATO SOUP
WITH PESTO OIL

This soup takes me back to the time when I was living in London and working at the most beautiful cookbook store in Notting Hill: Books for Cooks. There was a little cafe at the back of the bookstore where I would bake bread, whip up cakes, and make nourishing soups to take the sting out of London's cold winter days.

SERVES 4

SOUP

10 tomatoes

2 onions, quartered

4 garlic cloves, smashed

2 sprigs of fresh thyme

3 tablespoons coconut oil, melted, or extra-virgin olive oil

2 tablespoons apple cider vinegar or balsamic vinegar

Pink salt

Freshly ground black pepper

1 cup fresh basil leaves

PESTO OIL

1 cup fresh basil leaves

½ cup macadamia nuts, soaked (see page 50)

¼ cup extra-virgin olive oil

½ teaspoon pink salt

Freshly ground black pepper

Preheat the oven to 375°F. Line a baking sheet with parchment paper.

Using a sharp knife, cut a cross into the bottom of each tomato and place cross side up on the prepared baking sheet. Add the onions, garlic and thyme, then drizzle with the coconut oil and apple cider vinegar. Sprinkle with salt and black pepper. Bake for about 30 minutes, until very soft. Allow to cool slightly.

Remove the thyme and discard. Transfer the roasted vegetables and all their liquid into a blender, add the basil, and blend on high speed until smooth and creamy. Taste, and adjust seasonings if needed.

To make the pesto oil, put all the ingredients into a food processor and pulse until the macadamias are finely chopped and the mixture oozy—you want a little texture to the oil.

To serve, ladle the soup into bowls or mugs and top each with a spoonful of the pesto oil.

VEGETABLE NOODLES
IN A SPICY MISO LEMONGRASS BROTH

This delicious vegetable-noodle soup is the perfect staple for colder weather. My fixation with raw vegetable noodles is no secret, and adding them to a nourishing miso soup was a no-brainer! The delicate strands of vegetables complement the healing miso broth. Don't forget: be careful not to boil miso or you will lose some of its amazing benefits.

SERVES 4

Spiralizer

8 cups water

2 lemongrass stalks, tender yellow parts only, sliced thin

2 tablespoons minced fresh ginger

2 garlic cloves, minced

¼ cup white miso

4 baby bok choy, cut in half

1 carrot, spiralized

1 zucchini, spiralized

¼ cup dry arame

2 tablespoons dry wakame broken into small pieces

2 tablespoons Bragg Liquid Aminos or tamari

1 tablespoon plus 1½ teaspoons sesame oil

4 green onions, finely chopped

2 tablespoons chopped fresh cilantro

2 tablespoons sesame seeds or hulled hemp seeds

1 long green chili pepper, sliced thin, for garnish

Handful of sprouted beans or seeds of choice, for garnish (see page 31)

Combine the water, lemongrass, ginger, and garlic in a large saucepan over medium heat and bring to a boil. Turn off the heat. Add the miso and stir until incorporated. Add the bok choy, carrot, zucchini, arame, wakame, Liquid Aminos, and sesame oil, and stir to combine. Add the green onions, cilantro, and sesame seeds. Warm gently over a low flame if necessary.

To serve, divide the soup between four bowls and garnish with the chili pepper and sprouts.

NOURISHING SEA BROTH

Broths are so healing and easy to digest. You can make them with all sorts of vegetables, but be sure to use kombu and shiitake as the base. They both contain beneficial properties that boost the immune system, nourish the brain, and offer a unique depth of flavor.

MAKES ABOUT 2½ QUARTS

10 cups water

8 dried kombu strips

1 cup dried shiitake mushrooms, sliced or whole

1 celery stalk, chopped

2 shallots, skin removed and quartered

2 tablespoons apple cider vinegar

1 tablespoon chopped fresh ginger

1 tablespoon chopped fresh turmeric

Small handful of fresh cilantro, whole

2 tablespoons sesame oil

3 green onions, sliced

⅓ cup chopped fresh cilantro

2 garlic cloves, crushed

2 tablespoons miso

2 tablespoons tamari

Bring the water to a boil in a large pot. Add the kombu, shiitakes, celery, shallots, cider vinegar, ginger, turmeric, and cilantro leaves and stems. Reduce the heat to low, cover, and simmer for 1 hour. Strain the liquid, reserving the kombu and mushrooms, and return the liquid to the pot.

Heat the sesame oil in a small skillet over medium heat. Add the green onions, chopped cilantro, and garlic, and sauté until fragrant, about 1 minute. Add the green onion mixture to the pot with the strained liquid. Take the pot off the heat, add the miso and tamari, and stir until the miso is incorporated.

You can slice the kombu and add it to the broth and the shiitakes if you like, or leave it as is. Ladle into bowls and enjoy.

BUTTERNUT SQUASH
APPLE SOUP
WITH GINGER & SAGE

I steam the squash for this soup to retain all of its nutrients. Butternut squash is a true beauty saver, rich in carotenoids—the pigments responsible for its vibrant orange color. These potent phytonutrients promote a glowing complexion and may help to protect the skin from ultraviolet damage. Butternuts are also packed with vitamins and minerals, including vitamin A, which is essential for healthy skin and eyes.

I find that steaming also makes the soup taste more vibrant, but if you prefer, you can sauté all the vegetables and herbs in a pot with a little coconut oil or ghee and then add water to cook.

SERVES 4

8 cups water	2 tablespoons raw honey
1 butternut squash, cut into 1-inch cubes	2 tablespoons extra-virgin olive oil
1 onion, chopped	2 tablespoons tamari
1 apple, chopped	1 teaspoon ground turmeric
¼ cup minced fresh ginger	1 teaspoon ground cinnamon
2 garlic cloves	Pink salt (optional)
1 red chili pepper	Freshly ground black pepper
4 fresh sage leaves	½ cup minced fresh cilantro, for garnish

Pour the water into a soup pot. Place a basket steamer into the soup pot and bring the water to a boil. Put the butternut squash pieces into the steamer and cover the pot. Steam for 5 to 12 minutes, until a fork pierces them easily. (The smaller the cubes, the less time is necessary to steam.) Turn off the heat. Remove the steamer from the pot and transfer the butternut pieces to a blender. Set aside.

Add the onion, apple, ginger, garlic, chili pepper, and sage to the hot water in the pot. Cover the pot and let stand for 10 minutes. When the water is cool enough, add everything to the blender along with the honey, olive oil, tamari, turmeric, and cinnamon. Blend on high speed until smooth and creamy. Taste, and season with salt if needed and black pepper to taste. Serve topped with minced cilantro.

132

GREEN GODDESS NOODLES

Turning vegetables into noodles creates wonderful texture and gives visual beauty to a dish. If you don't already own a spiralizer, drop what you're doing and buy yourself one. Throw in all types of hard vegetables and fruit, whirl it around, and welcome yourself into a whole new world. These noodles transform any dish from plain boring to breathtaking, both visually and texture wise, and they always upgrade a salad.

SERVES 4

Spiralizer

Bunch of kale

¼ cup fresh parsley, minced

2 tablespoons Bragg Liquid Aminos or tamari

2 tablespoons freshly squeezed lemon juice

1 tablespoon extra-virgin olive oil

1 teaspoon lemon zest

1 garlic clove, minced

Pinch of pink salt

1 beet, spiralized

1 cucumber, spiralized (try to avoid seeds)

1 avocado, diced

½ cup pumpkin seeds

2 tablespoons sesame seeds

2 cups Green Goddess Dressing (recipe follows)

Tear the kale into bite-size pieces and put into a big bowl. Add the Liquid Aminos, lemon juice, olive oil, lemon zest, garlic, and salt. Massage the kale with your hands for a couple of minutes to soften and coat.

Divide the dressed kale among four bowls. Top with the spiralized beet and cucumber and the avocado, distributing the ingredients evenly among the bowls. Sprinkle with the seeds, generously drizzle with the dressing, and serve.

(Continued)

135

GREEN GODDESS DRESSING

MAKES ABOUT 2 CUPS

1 avocado

¼ cup tahini

¼ cup extra-virgin olive oil

¼ cup water

¼ cup loosely packed fresh basil leaves

¼ cup loosely packed fresh parsley

¼ cup apple cider vinegar

3 tablespoons freshly squeezed lemon juice

2 tablespoons chopped chives

½ teaspoon spirulina

1 tablespoon Bragg Liquid Aminos or tamari

1 garlic clove

Pinch of pink salt

Pinch of freshly ground black pepper

Combine all the ingredients in a blender and blend on high speed until smooth and creamy, adding more water if necessary to achieve the desired consistency.

WATERCRESS RASPBERRY SALAD WITH MACADAMIA FETA
& ORANGE MAPLE DRESSING

Raspberries not only look great but their taste makes them a real gem: they're sweet, but with an arresting tartness. It's this tartness that makes them so perfect for this salad with its sweet, creamy maple dressing and rich, punchy macadamia feta.

SERVES 4

FETA

¼ cup macadamia nuts, soaked (see page 50)

2 tablespoons pine nuts

1 tablespoon freshly squeezed lemon juice

1 tablespoon apple cider vinegar

1 teaspoon lemon zest

1 teaspoon extra-virgin olive oil

1 tablespoon nutritional yeast

1 small garlic clove, minced

1 teaspoon pink salt

SALAD

4 cups watercress sprigs

Bunch of radishes, sliced thin

2 small cucumbers, sliced thin lengthways

1 avocado, sliced

1 pint fresh raspberries

TO SERVE

¼ cup soaked macadamias, chopped (see page 50)

Freshly ground black pepper

½ cup Orange Maple Dressing (recipe follows)

To make the feta, put the macadamia nuts and pine nuts into a food processor and pulse to make a fine meal. Add the lemon juice, cider vinegar, lemon zest, and olive oil, and pulse, scraping down the walls of the food processor as necessary with a rubber spatula, until smooth and well combined. Add the nutritional yeast, garlic, and salt, and pulse until crumbly.

To prepare the salad, put the watercress, radishes, cucumbers, avocado, and raspberries into a large bowl and toss to combine.

To serve, divide the salad among four bowls, top with the macadamias, a few turns of freshly ground black pepper, and a drizzle of the dressing. Crumble the feta on top and serve.

(Continued)

137

ORANGE MAPLE DRESSING

MAKES 1 CUP

¼ cup fresh orange juice

¼ cup extra-virgin olive oil

¼ cup apple cider vinegar

2 tablespoons maple syrup

2 tablespoons mustard of choice

¼ teaspoon ground cinnamon

Pinch of pink salt

Combine all the ingredients in a blender and blend on high speed until emulsified. Add more salt to taste if needed.

CRUNCHY SLAW
WITH CHIA DRESSING

This colorful crunchy slaw is filled with unexpected sweetness from the digestive-booster pineapple and antioxidant-rich basil. It will forever change your idea of coleslaw.

SERVES 4

2 cups shredded white cabbage

2 cups shredded red cabbage

½ pineapple, sliced thin

2 cups Chia Dressing (recipe follows)

1 cup loosely packed fresh basil leaves

½ cup unsweetened coconut chips

2 green onions, sliced thin

Put the white and red cabbage, the pineapple, and the dressing in a large bowl and toss to combine. Transfer the slaw to a serving dish and top with the basil, coconut chips, and green onion.

CHIA DRESSING

MAKES 2 CUPS

1 tablespoon lime zest

2 tablespoons freshly squeezed lime juice

1 cup plain unsweetened coconut milk yogurt

1 cup Cashew Sour Cream (page 203)

1 tablespoon chia seeds

Put all the ingredients in a bowl and whisk to combine. Taste and adjust seasonings if needed.

PAPAYA LIME SALAD
WITH CUCUMBER NOODLES
& RASPBERRY DRESSING

This summery, beauty-nutrient-dense papaya salad is a crowd favorite, and it's a great meal for hot days when you don't want to go near the stove. This Thai-inspired salad is packed with collagen-producing beta-carotene—perfect for giving you a little added protection from the dehydrating effects of the sun.

SERVES 4

Julienne Peeler

1 cup baby lettuce leaves

1 ripe papaya, cut into wedges

1 avocado, cubed

1 cucumber, shredded using a julienne peeler

1 cup Raspberry Dressing (recipe follows)

1 red chili pepper, finely sliced

⅓ cup loosely packed fresh mint leaves

⅓ cup fresh cilantro leaves

⅓ cup fresh basil leaves, shredded

¼ cup Rosemary Garlic Macadamias (page 184) or Sweet & Spicy Cashews (page 183)

1 lime, cut into thin slices with a mandoline

Divide the lettuce, papaya, avocado, and cucumber evenly among four bowls. Drizzle with the raspberry dressing. Top with the chili, mint, cilantro, basil, and macadamias or cashews, distributing the ingredients evenly among the bowls. Top with the lime slices and serve.

(Continued)

RASPBERRY DRESSING

MAKES ABOUT I CUP

1 cup raspberries

½ cup fresh orange juice

¼ cup beet juice

¼ cup olive oil

2 tablespoons apple cider vinegar

1 garlic clove, chopped

1 tablespoon lemon juice

1 tablespoon honey or sweetener of choice

1 teaspoon Dijon mustard

Pinch of pink salt

Pinch of freshly ground black pepper

Place all the ingredients in a blender and blend until smooth and creamy. Taste and adjust seasoning with salt and pepper if desired.

INTO THE SEA SALAD BOWL
WITH ORANGE DRESSING

A perfect way to introduce more seaweed into your diet, this delicious bowl has an array of beautifying benefits. Sea vegetables are full of iodine, a powerful nutrient that supports the thyroid gland. When your thyroid is out of whack, your mood, cognitive function, and weight are affected—and it can cause dry skin, brittle hair and nails, liquid retention, and puffy skin, and fine lines and wrinkles appear earlier and become more noticeable. This is where sea vegetables come in! Consuming them regularly supports your glands that produce and regulate hormones, helping to balance mood, weight, and vitality and create beautiful, youthful skin.

SERVES 4

¼ cup plus 1 tablespoon dried hijiki

¾ cup water

2 cups cooked quinoa

3 carrots, peeled and shredded

1 cup loosely packed fresh cilantro leaves

1 cup soaked almonds (see page 50)

2 tablespoons sesame seeds

1 cup Orange Dressing (recipe follows)

1 ripe avocado, cubed

In a small bowl, soak the dried hijiki in ¾ cup of water for about 15 minutes. Drain well.

In a large bowl, toss the reconstituted hijiki, and the quinoa, carrots, cilantro, almonds, and sesame seeds to combine. Add the dressing and toss to coat. Divide the salad among four bowls, top with the avocado, and serve.

(Continued)

ORANGE DRESSING

MAKES ½ CUP

¼ cup fresh orange juice

2 tablespoons extra-virgin olive oil

2 tablespoons brown rice vinegar
or apple cider vinegar

1 tablespoon tamari

1 tablespoon toasted sesame oil

1 tablespoon coconut sugar
or raw honey

1 garlic clove, crushed

1 teaspoon mustard of choice

In a medium bowl, whisk together all the ingredients until incorporated.

MANGO & AVOCADO CEVICHE

Inspired by Polynesian ceviche, which uses loads of lime juice and coconut cream, my fishless version has all the taste and many more nutrients. It is great served with gluten-free coconut tortilla chips to scoop it up.

SERVES 4

2 avocados

1 lime, cut into wedges

2 small mangos (or 1 medium)

2 tomatoes, seeded and diced

1 small red onion, finely chopped

1 cup corn

1 cup unsweetened coconut milk or plant milk of choice

2 green onions, chopped

½ cup freshly squeezed lime juice

½ cup coarsely chopped fresh cilantro

1 jalapeño, finely diced

1 tablespoon sesame seeds

Pink salt

Coconut tortilla chips (optional)

Cut the avocados in half and remove the pits. Scoop out the center of the flesh onto a board, leaving a ½-inch layer around the inside of each avocado half to act as a bowl. Squeeze lime over the insides of the "bowls" to prevent discoloration.

Coarsely chop the scooped-out avocado flesh and put into a medium bowl. Add the mangos, tomatoes, red onion, corn, coconut milk, green onions, lime juice, cilantro, jalapeño, and sesame seeds and toss to combine. Add salt to taste. Let the ceviche sit for 5 minutes for the flavors to develop.

Divide ceviche among four bowls and serve with coconut tortilla chips, if desired.

WILD RICE MUSHROOM TARTARE

This salad featuring nutty, flavored wild rice—which, of course, is highly nutritious and gluten free—makes an elegant entree. Wild rice isn't actually a rice but a water-grass seed, and although you can't sprout wild rice, you can "bloom" it. During this process the seeds soaked in water actually unfold, very much like little petals, revealing their pale, tender insides. Soaking makes the protein and all the nutrients more bioavailable, and it makes this recipe delicious!

SERVES 4

MARINATED MUSHROOMS

3 cups thinly sliced shiitake mushrooms

2 tablespoons sesame oil

2 tablespoons Bragg Liquid Aminos or tamari

2 tablespoons umeboshi plum vinegar or balsamic vinegar

1 tablespoon grated fresh ginger

Pinch of pink salt

WILD RICE MIXTURE

¼ cup plus 1 tablespoon dried hijiki

¾ cups water

2½ cups "bloomed" wild rice (see note)

¼ cup raspberries

¼ cup almonds or cashews, soaked and chopped (see page 50)

¼ cup chopped fresh mint

2 tablespoons chopped chives

2 tablespoons extra-virgin olive oil

1 garlic clove, minced

TO SERVE

1 cup loosely packed microgreens

½ cup Raspberry Dressing (page 144)

Tip: Rinse the rice well and put it in a glass jar covered with filtered water. Let it soak on the counter overnight. In the morning, drain and rinse the rice, then cover it with fresh water and put it in the fridge. Drain and rinse the rice at least twice a day for 2 to 3 days until the rice has "bloomed"—some or all of the grains will have split open, and it should be tender to eat.

To marinate the mushrooms, whisk together the sesame oil, Liquid Aminos, umeboshi vinegar, ginger, and salt in a medium bowl. Add the mushrooms and toss to coat. Let marinate for at least 30 minutes. To make the wild rice mixture, cover the hijiki with the water in a small bowl and let soak for 15 minutes. Drain well.

In a big bowl, toss the wild rice, soaked hijiki, raspberries, almonds, mint, chives, olive oil, and garlic to combine. To serve, top the wild rice mixture with the marinated mushrooms and microgreens and drizzle with the raspberry dressing.

INDIAN SALAD BOWL
WITH CRUNCHY CHICKPEAS
& MANGO CHUTNEY

This fresh and vibrant Indian-inspired salad bowl and its gorgeous mango chutney are packed with wrinkle-eliminating nutrients. Chickpeas are very rich in manganese, which enhances skin health and reduces fine lines and wrinkles by helping the skin to combat free radicals, providing a supple, radiant complexion.

SERVES 4

Julienne Peeler

CRUNCHY CHICKPEAS

2 tablespoons coconut oil or ghee

1 tablespoon curry powder

2 teaspoons smoked paprika

1 teaspoon ground cumin

Pinch of pink salt

1 cup sprouted chickpeas (see page 31)

¼ cup unsweetened shredded coconut

MANGO CHUTNEY

2 firm ripe mangoes, diced

2 tablespoons finely chopped fresh cilantro

1 tablespoon grated fresh ginger

2 teaspoons cayenne (add more to turn up the heat!)

2 teaspoons apple cider vinegar

¼ teaspoon ground cumin

Pinch of pink salt

Freshly ground black pepper

SALAD

2 cups salad mix

1 cup cherry tomatoes, cut in half

1 large carrot, shredded using a julienne peeler

½ cucumber, seeded and diced

Handful of fresh cilantro leaves

Handful of mint leaves

2 tablespoons freshly squeezed lemon juice

1 tablespoon extra-virgin olive oil

2 teaspoons raw honey

To make the crunchy chickpeas, heat a large skillet over medium-high heat. Add the coconut oil, curry powder, paprika, cumin, and salt, and cook for 2 minutes. Add the sprouted chickpeas and coconut, and cook until the chickpeas are golden, 2 to 3 minutes. Set aside.

To make the mango chutney, put the mangoes, cilantro, ginger, cayenne, cider vinegar, cumin, and salt into a medium bowl and gently fold together to combine. Add more salt and freshly ground black pepper to taste.

To make the salad, toss the salad mix, tomatoes, carrot, cucumber, cilantro, mint, lemon juice, olive oil, and honey to combine. Divide the salad among four bowls. Top each salad with some warm crunchy chickpeas and a dollop of mango chutney.

MOROCCAN SPICED SQUASH SALAD
WITH CHICKPEA POPCORN

I am crazy about winter squash in any shape or form, so love dishes that highlight this amazing sweet vegetable. This hearty, heartwarming, Moroccan-inspired salad served with crunchy spiced chickpeas is just what you'll be craving when the temperature dips.

SERVES 4

1 butternut squash, cut into wedges

2 tablespoons coconut oil or ghee, melted

1 teaspoon ground cinnamon

1 teaspoon whole cumin seeds

1 teaspoon smoked paprika

Pinch of pink salt

1 large handful fresh sage leaves

2 garlic cloves, peeled

¾ cup sprouted chickpeas (see page 31)

Preheat the oven to 400°F. Put the squash on a baking sheet, add the coconut oil, and toss to coat. Sprinkle the squash wedges with the cinnamon, cumin, paprika, and salt. Add the sage and garlic, and toss until the squash is evenly coated with the spices. Bake for 10 minutes.

Remove the baking sheet from the oven, add the chickpeas, and toss to coat them with the roasting juices. Return the pan to the oven and bake for 15 minutes more, or until tender, and serve immediately.

SNACKS

Clean eating doesn't have to be boring. Here are some of my favorite healthy snacks—they are satisfying without making you feel sluggish, and will keep you on the right track between meals. We often hear that snacking is bad for you, but that's not always true. If you're eating the right snack, it will do just what it needs to do: keep you from being distracted by hunger and boost your energy level.

RAINBOW ROLLS

I have fond memories of learning to roll these delicate rice paper rolls when I was working at Mana Foods, a local and organic grocery store on Maui. There was an amazingly strong lady in charge of assembling these rolls for the deli section, and she was a pro. The rolls at Mana Foods were filled with noodles, tofu, and a big dollop of hoisin sauce. My version includes a creamy Thai almond sauce and an array of spiralized vegetables to make it look like a rainbow when you bite in. They are a great way to eat the rainbow!

MAKES 4

Spiralizer

ALMOND SAUCE

½ cup chopped fresh cilantro

¼ cup water

Up to ½ cup almond butter

3 tablespoons Bragg Liquid Aminos or tamari

2 tablespoons freshly squeezed lime juice

1 tablespoon apple cider vinegar

1 tablespoon raw honey or maple syrup

2 Medjool dates, pitted

1 garlic clove

1 tablespoon grated fresh ginger

1 teaspoon red pepper flakes

¼ cup macadamias, soaked and crushed (see page 50)

ROLLS

4 rice paper wrappers

1 cucumber, spiralized or grated (try to avoid the seeds)

1 avocado, sliced

1 cup spiralized or grated beets

1 cup spiralized or grated carrots

1 cup sprouts

½ cup fresh cilantro leaves

½ cup loosely packed fresh mint leaves

¼ cup loosely packed fresh basil leaves

To make the almond sauce, combine the cilantro, water, almond butter, Liquid Aminos, lime juice, cider vinegar, honey, dates, garlic, ginger, and red pepper flakes in a blender and blend on high speed until smooth, adding more water if necessary to achieve a pourable (but still thick) sauce. Divide the sauce evenly between two small bowls. Set aside one bowl (half the sauce) for dipping. Stir the crushed macadamias into the other bowl of sauce and set aside for filling the rolls.

(Continued)

158

To prepare the rolls, fill a wide, shallow bowl with warm water and place a clean, dry dish towel on your work surface. Submerge a rice paper wrapper in the water just until soft. (Do not oversoak: the wrappers are delicate and will tear if too soft.) Remove the wrapper from the water and place on the dish towel.

Arrange one quarter of the vegetables and herbs horizontally in the bottom third of the wrapper, leaving the sides and top section of the wrapper uncovered. Dollop 1 tablespoon of the macadamia almond sauce over the vegetables. Fold the bottom edge of the wrapper over the veggies and herbs and tuck it under them. Fold the sides of the wrapper toward the middle (like wrapping a burrito), then gently roll it closed as tightly as possible without tearing. Cover the finished roll with a damp cloth to keep it moist. Repeat the process with the remaining fillings and wrappers. Serve accompanied by the almond dipping sauce.

NO RICE SUSHI

A sushi roll without rice is not what you'd expect, but that's a good thing. Filled with a delicious ginger almond pâté and a variety of vegetables, these rolls will boost your skin's moisture and elasticity. Almonds are high in vitamin E, which keeps your skin moisturized and helps protect against ultraviolet rays. Vegetables in their raw state are full of water—some as much as 95 percent (cucumber)—so you're not only getting tons of vitamins and minerals, but you're basically "eating your water" as well.

MAKES 4 ROLLS
OF 6 PIECES EACH

GINGER ALMOND SPREAD

½ cup almond butter

2 tablespoons white miso

1 tablespoon umeboshi plum paste

1 tablespoon apple cider vinegar

1 tablespoon Bragg Liquid Aminos
or tamari

1 tablespoon raw honey or maple syrup

¼ cup sesame seeds

2 tablespoons grated fresh ginger

2 tablespoons finely chopped
green onion

1 garlic clove, finely minced

Pinch of cayenne (optional)

4 sheets nori

VEGETABLES FOR FILLING

1 avocado, sliced

½ cucumber, cut in matchsticks

½ carrot, cut in matchsticks

½ cup shredded red cabbage

¼ cup red bell pepper, cut in matchsticks

TO SERVE

Bragg Liquid Aminos

Pickled Ginger (recipe follows)

To make the spread, stir together the almond butter, miso, umeboshi paste, cider vinegar, Liquid Aminos, and honey in a medium bowl. Add the sesame seeds, ginger, green onion, garlic, and cayenne, if using, and stir well to combine. The filling should be quite thick.

(Continued)

To assemble, place 1 sheet of nori, shiny side down, on a sushi mat. (If you don't have a mat, you can use a kitchen towel or place it directly on your work surface.) Smear 3 tablespoons of the spread evenly across the bottom third of the nori sheet, leaving 1 inch of the sheet exposed at the bottom but spreading all the way to the edge on the left and right sides. Lay about a quarter of the filling vegetables in a horizontal line on top of the spread. For a nice touch, extend the vegetables ½ inch past the sides of the nori sheet to create decorative end pieces.

Moisten the top edge of the nori with a little water. Carefully lift the edge closest to you up and over the filling and squeeze firmly in place. Lift your end of the mat up and use it to help you continue rolling until you reach the moistened nori and seal the roll. Wrap the mat around the whole roll and squeeze gently to secure. Remove the roll from the mat and place it seam-side down. (Alternatively, use your hands to firmly and evenly roll up the sushi.) Use a moistened knife to slice it into 6 pieces. Repeat with remaining ingredients and nori.

PICKLED GINGER

MAKES I CUP

¼ cup raw honey

2 tablespoons coconut nectar

1 tablespoon beet juice

1 tablespoon Bragg Liquid Aminos or tamari

2 teaspoons pink salt

1 cup peeled and thinly sliced fresh ginger

In a medium bowl, stir together the honey, coconut nectar, beet juice, Liquid Aminos, and salt to combine. Add the ginger and gently toss to coat. Transfer the ginger and liquid into a clean glass jar with a lid. Cover and allow to marinate for at least 1 day. The pickled ginger will keep fresh for weeks in the refrigerator.

CHEESY PESTO CHIPS

These chips are addictive—they're so cheesy, crunchy, and delicious. I like to cut the zucchini into thin slices so they get extra crisp. The creaminess of the macadamia nuts lends itself perfectly to cheesy pesto, with the added bonus that macadamias contain a high concentration of palmitoleic acid—an antiaging nutrient that immensely benefits the skin and cell turnover and that is present in all human tissues, especially the liver. Because palmitoleic acid gets depleted quickly as skin ages, it is important to refuel with outside sources, and macadamias are a great one.

SERVES 4

Dehydrator (optional)

MACADAMIA PESTO

2 cups loosely packed
fresh basil leaves

1 cup macadamia nuts, soaked
(see page 50)

2 garlic cloves

3 tablespoons extra-virgin olive oil

1 tablespoon nutritional yeast

½ teaspoon pink salt

3 zucchinis

To make the pesto, pulse all the pesto ingredients in a food processor until everything is well incorporated but not completely smooth. Set aside.

Slice the unpeeled zucchinis into thin rounds using a mandoline or sharp knife. Spread a dollop of the pesto over a slice, smear with the back of a spoon, and place on a mesh dehydrator tray. Repeat with the remaining zucchini slices and pesto, covering each dehydrator tray in a single layer of zucchini slices. Dehydrate for 10 hours or until crisp (page 59). Alternatively, you can bake the chips in a 400°F preheated oven for 10 to 15 minutes, until golden. Stored in an airtight container at room temperature, these will keep for up to 1 week.

NORI CHIPS

I am such a seaweed lover. My kids are really into the salty taste of sea vegetables too, but I've found that nori is their favorite. I came up with this recipe as a cheeky way to get them to eat more. The topping is flavorful—and colorful, thanks to the turmeric. Work quickly when making these chips so the wet topping doesn't sit too long on the nori—nori tends to shrink in contact with moisture.

SERVES 4

Dehydrator

20 nori sheets

2 cups macadamia nuts, soaked
(see page 50)

1½ cups water

2 tablespoons freshly squeezed
lemon juice

2 tablespoons nutritional yeast

1 garlic clove

1 teaspoon pink salt

1 teaspoon turmeric

Cut the nori sheets into bite-size pieces. Place them in a single layer on mesh dehydrator trays and set aside.

Combine the macadamias, water, lemon juice, nutritional yeast, garlic, pink salt, and turmeric in a blender and blend on high speed until smooth and creamy. Using a spoon, dollop a bit of the mixture on each piece of nori and smear it with the back of the spoon. Dehydrate for about 12 hours, or until crisp (see page 59). Stored in an airtight container at room temperature, nori chips will keep for up to 2 weeks.

SAVORY SPIRULINA POPCORN

Who doesn't like popcorn? In my house we are divided between sweet and salty, so I make a salty and a sweet version to keep everyone happy! Green popcorn is always a hit too—maybe it's the color, or maybe it's the addictive cheesy flavor, and how healthy can you get?! Don't be put off by the idea of spirulina on popcorn, because if you don't know by now, spirulina is considered one of the world's most nutrient-dense superfoods. Spirulina is packed with proteins, vitamins (especially vitamins A, B12, and E), minerals, and fatty acids, and it's prized for its ability to treat aging skin and dark circles under the eyes.

SERVES 4 TO 6

1 tablespoon coconut oil

½ cup popcorn kernels

2 tablespoons nutritional yeast

1 to 2 teaspoons spirulina

1 teaspoon minced fresh thyme

1 teaspoon minced fresh rosemary

1 teaspoon pink salt

½ garlic clove, finely minced (optional)

Melt the coconut oil in a medium heavy-bottomed pot over high heat. Add the popcorn kernels and cover with a lid. Give the pot a good shake every 10 seconds as it's popping so the popcorn doesn't burn. When you hear the popping stop, remove the pot from the heat and dump the popped corn into a large bowl.

Sprinkle the popcorn with the nutritional yeast, spirulina, thyme, rosemary, salt, and garlic, if using, and toss well to coat. Allow the popcorn to cool slightly then enjoy! If you have any left over, it can be stored in an airtight container for up to 3 days.

TOFFEE MACA POPCORN

We have been making this version of oven-baked caramel popcorn for a while, which mimics the sugary clusters of its not-so-healthy counterpart. There have been some sticky burnt fingers, though—be careful to let the popcorn cool down a bit after removing it from the oven. It is well worth the wait.

SERVES 4 TO 6

1 tablespoon coconut oil

½ cup popcorn kernels

¼ cup plus 1 tablespoon maple syrup

1 tablespoon almond butter

1 tablespoon cacao powder

1 teaspoon maca powder

1 teaspoon mesquite powder

1 teaspoon ground cinnamon

1 teaspoon pink salt

½ teaspoon ground cardamom

½ teaspoon vanilla bean powder

¼ cup almonds or walnuts, soaked (see page 50)

Preheat the oven to 320°F. Line a baking tray with parchment paper and set aside.

Melt the coconut oil in a medium heavy-bottomed pot over high heat. Add the popcorn kernels and cover with a lid. Give the pot a good shake every 10 seconds as it's popping so the popcorn doesn't burn. When you hear the popping stop, remove the pot from the heat and dump the popped corn into a large bowl.

Combine the maple syrup, almond butter, cacao, maca, and mesquite powders, cinnamon, salt, cardamom, and vanilla powder in a blender and blend on high speed until incorporated.

Add the almonds to the popcorn. Add the blended mixture and toss to coat. Spread the coated popcorn and almonds over the prepared baking sheet and bake for 6 minutes. Rotate the baking sheet and bake for another 2 to 3 more minutes, until crisp and golden.

Remove from the oven and sprinkle with pink salt. Allow the caramel popcorn to cool slightly on the baking sheet, then enjoy! If you have any left over, it can be stored in an airtight container for up to 3 days.

HOMEMADE
NUT CHEESES & CRACKERS

These are tried and true nut cheese recipes. Even cheese purists love them. And every cheese deserves to be served on some good crackers—these crackers are the perfect companion, lightly seasoned so as not to upstage the cheeses.

BASIC NUT CHEESE

Flavor is gained by letting this nut cheese mature for longer before refrigerating—it becomes tangier, with more depth. If instead you prefer a milder taste that resembles cream cheese, refrigerate immediately.

MAKES 3 CUPS

Dehydrator (optional)

2 cups cashews, soaked
(see page 50)

1 cup macadamia nuts, soaked

1 cup water

2 teaspoons white miso, or
1 teaspoon probiotic powder

Line a sieve with a piece of folded cheesecloth or an open nut bag and place over a bowl. Locate a small plate that will fit inside the rim of the sieve and set aside.

Combine the cashews, macadamia nuts, and water in a blender and blend on high until completely smooth. Stir in the miso. Scoop the mixture into the lined sieve. If using cheesecloth, next fold the cloth edges snugly over the mixture and then turn over the parcel, setting it back into the sieve so that the cloth edges are sealed and no mixture can escape. If using a nut bag, twist the opening to seal it. Position the small plate over the parcel in the sieve and carefully put a weight on top to help drain the "whey" from the cheese. Incubate in the dehydrator at 85°F to 95°F for 24 hours. Alternatively, you can set everything on top of your stove with the oven set to the lowest temperature.

During this time the cheese will ferment: there should be some fluffiness to it, and it should no longer taste like only pureed nuts. If you are happy with the texture at this point, you can serve the cheese immediately. For a tangier cheese, let the cheese sit for longer. If not eating immediately, transfer the cheese into an airtight glass jar and store in the refrigerator for up to 2 weeks.

If you want a thicker cheese, transfer your cheese into cheese molds and freeze for 1 hour. Unmold the cheeses directly onto dehydrator sheets and dehydrate at 118°F for 12 hours, then flip the cheese rounds over and dehydrate for an additional 24 hours. You can store the cheese in the refrigerator for up to a month.

SUN-DRIED TOMATO NUT CHEESE

MAKES ABOUT 3½ CUPS

Dehydrator (optional)

¼ cup sun-dried tomatoes, soaked

3 cups Basic Nut Cheese
(page 175)

2 tablespoons chopped fresh basil

1 teaspoon chopped fresh thyme

1 teaspoon minced fresh rosemary

½ garlic clove, finely minced

1 teaspoon pink salt

½ teaspoon freshly ground black pepper

½ teaspoon freshly squeezed lemon juice

In a food processor, pulse the soaked tomatoes to finely chop. Add the basic nut cheese and the basil, thyme, rosemary, garlic, salt, pepper, and lemon juice and process into a smooth paste. If you are happy with the texture at this point, you can serve the cheese immediately.

If you want a thicker cheese, transfer your cheese into cheese molds and freeze for 1 hour. Unmold the cheeses directly onto dehydrator sheets and dehydrate at 118°F for 12 hours, then flip the cheese rounds over and dehydrate for an additional 24 hours. When the cheese is done, serve immediately or transfer into an airtight glass jar and store in the refrigerator for up to 2 weeks.

OLIVE OREGANO NUT CHEESE

MAKES ABOUT 4 CUPS

Dehydrator (optional)

3 cups Basic Nut Cheese (page 175)

1 cup black olives, pitted and chopped

¼ cup freshly squeezed lemon juice

2 tablespoons minced red onion

2 tablespoons minced fresh oregano

2 tablespoons extra-virgin olive oil

1 garlic clove, minced

2 teaspoons nutritional yeast

1 teaspoon pink salt

Put all the ingredients into a large bowl and stir well to combine. If you are happy with the texture at this point, you can serve the cheese immediately.

If you want a thicker cheese, transfer your cheese into cheese molds and freeze for 1 hour. Unmold the cheeses directly onto dehydrator sheets and dehydrate at 118°F for 12 hours, then flip the cheese rounds over and dehydrate for an additional 24 hours. When it is done, serve immediately or transfer into an airtight glass jar and store in the refrigerator for up to 2 weeks.

HERB & FLOWER NUT CHEESE

MAKES ABOUT 4 CUPS

Dehydrator (optional)

½ cup pine nuts

1 garlic clove

3 cups Basic Nut Cheese
(page 175)

2 teaspoons fresh thyme

2 teaspoons fresh marjoram

2 teaspoons fresh rosemary

½ teaspoon dried lavender

½ teaspoon dried calendula flowers

¼ cup freshly squeezed lemon juice

2 tablespoons extra-virgin olive oil

1 tablespoon apple cider vinegar

1 tablespoon raw honey

1 teaspoon pink salt

Pinch of freshly ground black pepper

In a food processor, pulse the pine nuts and garlic to finely chop. Add the basic cheese and the thyme, marjoram, rosemary, lavender, calendula, lemon juice, olive oil, cider vinegar, honey, salt, and black pepper, and process into a smooth paste. If you are happy with the texture at this point, you can serve the cheese immediately.

If you want a thicker cheese, transfer your cheese into cheese molds and freeze for 1 hour. Unmold the cheeses directly onto dehydrator sheets and dehydrate at 118°F for 12 hours, then flip the cheese rounds over and dehydrate for an additional 24 hours. When done, you can serve the cheese immediately or transfer into an airtight glass jar and store in the refrigerator for up to 2 weeks.

ALMOND AND HERB CRACKERS

MAKES 24 TO 36 CRACKERS

Dehydrator

½ shallot

1 garlic clove

½ cup water

2 cups almonds, soaked
(see page 50)

⅓ cup flaxseeds, finely ground

3 tablespoons extra-virgin olive oil

1 tablespoon fresh thyme leaves

1 tablespoon fresh rosemary leaves

1 tablespoon nutritional yeast

1 tablespoon freshly ground
black pepper

1 teaspoon pink salt

Line your dehydrator trays with nonstick baking sheets. Combine the shallot, garlic, and water in a blender and blend on high speed until smooth. Set aside.

Dry the almonds with a clean dish towel and put into a food processor. Process until the almonds are the consistency of chunky couscous. (If they are chopped too fine, the crackers will not have as nice a texture.) Transfer the ground almond into a medium bowl. Add the blended garlic mixture and the flaxseeds, olive oil, thyme, rosemary, nutritional yeast, black pepper, and salt and knead together with your hands until well combined. If the mixture is not coming together into a dough, add more water by the tablespoon as needed.

Spread half of the mixture evenly over a prepared dehydrator tray. Place a clean nonstick baking sheet or piece of parchment paper on top and use a rolling pin to roll out very thin. Score the mixture into rectangles 1 inch wide and 7 inches long. Repeat with the remaining dough.

Place the trays in the dehydrator and dehydrate for 24 hours (see page 59). Flip over the scored crackers, slide the nonstick sheets out from under them, and dehydrate on the mesh trays for another 24 hours. Break into separate crackers and let cool, then serve with nut cheese of your choice. You can store the crackers in an airtight container for up to 2 months.

ADDICTIVE NUTS

Sweet and salty and convenient, nuts are guilt-free and delicious beauty foods. Here's a selection of the most nourishing, energizing, and skin-loving nutty snacks for any occasion, any time of day, wherever you may be. It makes such a difference to your body when you show it love by feeding it the nutrients and good fats it craves, to fuel your day and your well-being.

COFFEE COCONUT MACADAMIAS

I love the taste of coffee in sweets, and as soon as I saw a coffee nut mixture at a roastery in Kauai, I knew I had to try them. This recipe recreates what I recall of that mellow, sweet concoction lightly spiced with coffee.

MAKES 4 CUPS

Dehydrator

½ cup maple syrup

¼ cup ground coffee

2 tablespoons unsweetened shredded coconut

2 tablespoons coconut sugar

1 teaspoon vanilla bean powder

1 teaspoon pink salt

4 cups macadamia nuts, soaked (see page 50)

Line 2 dehydrator trays with nonstick baking sheets. Put the maple syrup, ground coffee, coconut, coconut sugar, vanilla powder, and salt into a big bowl and stir until well combined. Add the macadamias and toss to coat. Distribute the nuts evenly in a single layer on the prepared trays. Dehydrate for 12 hours (see page 59). Break the mixture into small clumps and continue to dehydrate for 24 hours, or until the macadamia nuts have a candied texture. Let cool.

Stored in an airtight container at room temperature, these nuts will keep for up to 3 months.

SWEET & SPICY CASHEWS

I can eat these by the handful and never get tired. They are the perfect balance of sweet and spicy.

MAKES 4 CUPS

Dehydrator

¼ cup plus 1 tablespoon raw honey or maple syrup

2 teaspoons ground chipotle

2 teaspoons pink salt

1 teaspoon chili powder

4 cups cashews, soaked (see page 50)

Line 2 dehydrator trays with nonstick baking sheets. Put the honey, chipotle, salt, and chili powder into a big bowl and stir until well combined. Add the cashews and toss to coat. Transfer the mixture to the prepared dehydrator trays and loosely distribute, allowing it to form small clumps. Dehydrate for 12 hours (see page 59). Break the mixture into small clumps and continue to dehydrate for 24 hours, or until the cashews have a candied texture. Let cool.

Stored in an airtight container at room temperature, these nuts will keep for up to 3 months.

ROSEMARY GARLIC MACADAMIAS

These nuts make a great snack or salad topping. The combination of rosemary and garlic is a tried-and-true flavor that turns this snack addictive. As we all know, garlic is extremely antibacterial; not so well known is that garlic is also one of the best sources of sulfur, which is essential for the structure of skin, working with collagen to provide support. It also provides lipoic acid and taurine, which help rebuild collagen fibers that have been damaged. Rosemary is a natural astringent and has anti-inflammatory properties that help reduce redness and puffiness.

MAKES 4 CUPS

Dehydrator

3 tablespoons rosemary leaves, finely minced

3 tablespoons extra-virgin olive oil or macadamia oil

2 garlic cloves, finely minced

1 teaspoon ground chipotle

1 teaspoon pink salt

4 cups macadamia nuts, soaked (see page 50)

Line 2 dehydrator trays with nonstick baking sheets. Put the rosemary, olive oil, garlic, chipotle, and salt into a big bowl and stir until well combined. Add the macadamias and toss to coat. Transfer the mixture to the prepared dehydrator trays and loosely distribute, allowing it to form small clumps. Dehydrate for 12 hours (see page 59). Break the mixture into smaller clumps and continue to dehydrate for 24 hours, or until the macadamia nuts have a candied texture. Let cool.

Stored in an airtight container at room temperature, these nuts will keep for up to 3 months.

MAGICAL
CACAO ALMONDS

These almonds are truly magical, with hints of chocolate-y flavor from the cacao and cacao nibs, and notes of caramel from the maca and almond butter. The deliciousness is amplified by the natural sweetener mesquite, a low glycemic alternative that is also super rich in calcium for bone heath and magnesium to aid relaxation. Perfect for a late-night snack!

MAKES ABOUT 4 CUPS

Dehydrator

¾ cup maple syrup

1 tablespoon almond butter

1 tablespoon cacao powder

1 tablespoon maca powder

2 teaspoons mesquite powder

1 teaspoon vanilla bean powder

1 teaspoon ground cinnamon

1 teaspoon pink salt

4 cups almonds, soaked (see page 50)

¼ cup cacao nibs

Line 2 dehydrator trays with nonstick baking sheets. Combine the maple syrup, almond butter, cacao, maca, and mesquite powders, vanilla powder, cinnamon, and salt in a blender and blend on high speed until well combined. Combine the almonds and cacao nibs in a big bowl, add the blended mixture, and toss to coat. Transfer the mixture to the prepared dehydrator trays and loosely distribute, allowing it to form small clumps. Dehydrate for 12 hours (see page 59). Break the mixture into small clumps and continue to dehydrate for 24 hours, or until the almonds have a candied, nutlike texture. Let cool.

Stored in an airtight container at room temperature, these nuts will keep for up to 3 months.

MAIN MEALS

If you're anything like me, great conversation and delicious food are always a recipe for inspiration. I cook because I love to feed family and friends—I just love the connection and the incredible energy I get from cooking in a kitchen full of laughter and amazing smells. You really can't overestimate the importance of sitting down at the table and sharing your day. This is where we form intense bonds and create memories. Even if you only have a short time to eat your dinner, make a point of sitting down, relaxing, and enjoying your food and company (even if it's your own)—it will make all the difference to your digestion and your overall well-being.

LASAGNA PRIMAVERA

This is another favorite comfort food that I have given a complete makeover. There are a few steps involved, but the result is so impressive. I love to make this at the peak of summer, when the tomatoes are ripe and delicious and basil fragrant and abundant.

SERVES 6 TO 8

MARINATED MUSHROOMS

4 portobello mushrooms, caps only, chopped

2 garlic cloves, minced

1 shallot, minced

¼ cup extra-virgin olive oil

¼ cup Bragg Liquid Aminos or tamari

2 tablespoons freshly squeezed lemon juice or apple cider vinegar

2 sprigs of fresh thyme

Pinch of pink salt

Pinch of freshly ground black pepper

ZUCCHINI NOODLES

5 medium zucchinis

¼ cup freshly squeezed lemon juice

2 tablespoons extra-virgin olive oil

1 teaspoon pink salt

HERB RICOTTA

1½ cups macadamia nuts, soaked (see page 50)

½ cup water

¼ cup pine nuts, soaked

¼ cup loosely packed fresh basil leaves

2 tablespoons nutritional yeast

2 tablespoons freshly squeezed lemon juice

2 tablespoons extra-virgin olive oil

1 small garlic clove

1 teaspoon pink salt, or to taste

TOMATO MARINARA

2 cups seeded and chopped tomatoes

1½ cups sun-dried tomatoes, soaked

1 garlic clove

½ cup loosely packed fresh basil leaves

2 tablespoons extra-virgin olive oil

1 tablespoon raw honey, or 2 Medjool dates, pitted

1 tablespoon apple cider vinegar or freshly squeezed lemon juice

1 tablespoon loosely packed fresh oregano leaves

Pinch of red pepper flakes (optional)

Pinch of pink salt

Pinch of freshly ground black pepper

GARNISHES

Basil leaves, torn

Edible flowers, such as pansy or calendula

To marinate the mushrooms, toss together all the ingredients in a big bowl and set aside. Allow to marinate for 20 minutes to 1 hour.

To make the zucchini noodles, cut the ends off the zucchinis and cut in half lengthwise. Cut into thin, half-circle slices using a mandoline. Place in a shallow dish and drizzle with the lemon juice and the olive oil. Sprinkle with the salt and set aside to marinate while you make the herb ricotta.

To make the herb ricotta, combine all the ingredients in a blender and blend on high speed until creamy and fluffy, carefully adding water a little at a time as needed to achieve a ricotta-like consistency.

To make the tomato marinara, put all the ingredients into a blender and pulse to combine—don't blend until smooth. The sauce should have a little texture.

To assemble the lasagna, first drain the marinated mushrooms. Cover the base of a serving dish with a layer of zucchini slices, overlapping them slightly so there are no gaps. Spread with a layer of tomato marinara, then add some dollops of the herb ricotta and some of the drained mushrooms. Add another layer of zucchini and repeat the process until you run out of zucchini, finishing with a layer of marinara. Decorate with some torn basil leaves and edible flowers.

Allow the prepared lasagna to sit for at least 30 minutes to marry the flavors. The flavor improves with time, so feel free to let it sit for up to 1 day in the refrigerator before serving.

TAQUITOS WITH NACHO NUT CHEESE & MANGO SALSA

This is such a delicious meal—the cool mango salsa contrasts beautifully with the spicy taco meat. Lettuce leaves are used as the crunchy wraps for a light taste, and every bite of bundled-up salad bursts with flavors and textures. Make these when your family has the munchies, and watch them disappear.

SERVES 4

TACO MEAT

1 cup walnuts, soaked (see page 50)

½ celery stalk, finely chopped

½ carrot, grated

2 tablespoons minced fresh cilantro

Juice of 1 lime

1 tablespoon Bragg Liquid Aminos or tamari

1 teaspoon ground chipotle

1 teaspoon minced fresh oregano

½ teaspoon ground cumin

¼ teaspoon ground cinnamon

¼ teaspoon red pepper flakes

MANGO SALSA

2 mangos, diced

1 small red onion, minced

¼ cup minced fresh cilantro

2 to 3 tablespoons freshly squeezed lime juice

2 tablespoons minced fresh mint

1 garlic clove, crushed

½ teaspoon ground cumin

½ teaspoon pink salt

¼ teaspoon ground cayenne

NACHO NUT CHEESE

1 cup cashews, soaked (see page 50)

¼ cup chopped red bell pepper

¼ cup water

¼ cup freshly squeezed lemon juice

1 garlic clove

1 tablespoon nutritional yeast

1 teaspoon smoked paprika

1 teaspoon ground chipotle

½ teaspoon pink salt

¼ teaspoon turmeric

TO ASSEMBLE

8 iceberg lettuce leaves

2 avocados, sliced

1 cup fermented vegetables

⅓ cup chopped fresh cilantro

191

To make the taco meat, dry the walnuts with a clean dish towel and place in a food processor. Pulse until broken. Add the celery, carrot, cilantro, lime juice, Liquid Aminos, chipotle, oregano, cumin, cinnamon, and red pepper flakes, and pulse to combine. You want a coarse consistency.

To make the mango salsa, put all the ingredients into a medium bowl and stir to combine. Let stand for 10 minutes or more to allow the flavors to develop.

To make the nacho nut cheese, combine all the ingredients in a blender and blend on high speed until smooth and creamy. This cheese can be stored in an airtight container in the refrigerator for up to 2 weeks. If it gets too thick after chilling, add a little warm water to dilute it.

To assemble the taquitos, fill each lettuce leaf with some taco meat followed by mango salsa, sliced avocado, fermented veggies, and cilantro. Generously dollop some nacho cheese on top and enjoy!

MATCHA PESTO NOODLES
WITH CARAMELIZED TOMATOES

Light, refreshing, and effortless, this creamy veggie noodle bowl makes the perfect summertime lunch. In fact, an ideal combination of comfort food and health food, these noodles can be the building block for many summer meals. Piled high on top of farmer's market greens and topped with cilantro, sesame seeds, and fermented veggies, they pack maximum flavor and nutrients into one healthy bowl. The tomatoes need 12 hours to caramelize in the dehydrator, so start this recipe early, or make them ahead: they will keep for up to 1 week stored in an airtight container filled with olive oil and refrigerated.

SERVES 4

Spiralizer

MATCHA PESTO

2 cups loosely packed fresh basil leaves or fresh cilantro

1 avocado

½ cup macadamia nuts, soaked (optional; see page 50)

½ cup extra-virgin olive oil

¼ cup hemp seeds

2 garlic cloves

2 tablespoons freshly squeezed lime juice

1 teaspoon matcha

1 teaspoon pink salt, or to taste

Pinch of freshly ground black pepper

TO SERVE

Caramelized Tomatoes (recipe follows)

4 medium zucchini, spiralized

2 tablespoons sesame seeds (optional)

Prepare the caramelized tomatoes (see page 194).

To make the matcha pesto, combine all the ingredients in a food processor and pulse to incorporate into a sauce.

To serve, put the zucchini noodles into a big bowl. Pour the pesto over the noodles and toss to coat. Add the caramelized tomatoes and fold gently. Sprinkle with sesame seeds, if desired, and serve immediately, or leave the noodles to marinate in the juices for up to 20 minutes.

(Continued)

CARAMELIZED TOMATOES

MAKES 2 CUPS

Dehydrator

3 cups cherry tomatoes,
cut in half

½ cup extra-virgin olive oil

2 tablespoons balsamic vinegar

1 garlic clove, minced

1 tablespoon fresh thyme leaves

2 garlic cloves, minced

Pinch of pink salt

Pinch of freshly ground black pepper

Line a dehydrator tray with a nonstick baking sheet. Put all the ingredients into a large bowl and toss well to coat. Transfer the tomatoes onto the prepared dehydrator tray, drizzling them with any leftover juices. Dehydrate for 12 hours (see page 59). If not using right away, transfer the tomatoes to a covered container and store in the refrigerator for up to 1 week.

BEET RAVIOLI
WITH BASIL RICOTTA

This recipe is a stunner, and quick to whip up. It's creative vegan recipes like these that can make even the most carnivorous friend eager to try! Filled with a pillowy macadamia basil ricotta, these delicate beet ravioli make an impressive meal. Beet is known for its detoxification and liver-healing properties as well as helping to support collagen production, which is so essential to elasticity of the skin. The ricotta can be made up to a week ahead of time and stored in an airtight container in the fridge.

SERVES 4

BASIL RICOTTA

1½ cups macadamia nuts, soaked (see page 50)

½ cup cashews, soaked (see page 50)

¼ cup freshly squeezed lemon juice

3 tablespoons nutritional yeast

2 tablespoons extra-virgin olive oil (optional)

1 garlic clove, minced

1 teaspoon lemon zest

1 teaspoon pink salt, or to taste

1 cup loosely packed fresh basil leaves

RAVIOLI

2 large beets

2 tablespoons extra-virgin olive oil

1 tablespoon freshly squeezed lemon juice

Pinch of pink salt

Pinch of freshly ground black pepper

TO SERVE

2 tablespoons Basil Oil (recipe follows)

Microgreens, for garnish

To make the basil ricotta, combine the macadamias, cashews, lemon juice, nutritional yeast, olive oil, if using, garlic, lemon zest, and salt in a food processor and process until smooth. Add the basil and pulse to chop and just combine. Set aside.

To make the ravioli, use a mandoline to cut the beets into very thin slices. Place in a big bowl and drizzle with the olive oil and lemon juice and sprinkle with the salt and pepper. Toss to coat all the slices well.

To serve, lay one eighth of the beet slices on each of the four plates. Place a generous dollop of the basil ricotta onto each slice. Top each with another beet slice and press down gently to adhere to the ricotta. Drizzle with a little basil oil and garnish with microgreens.

196

BASIL OIL

MAKES ABOUT ½ CUP

1 cup basil leaves   ½ cup extra virgin olive oil

Put the basil leaves and olive oil in a blender and blend on high speed. Stored in a sealed glass jar, basil oil will keep for several weeks in the refrigerator.

MIDDLE EASTERN MEZZE

This Middle Eastern–inspired collection of dishes is vibrant, fresh, and perfect for a get-together. For a feast, serve the falafels with tabouli, beet and red pepper hummus, and tzatziki alongside. Offer lettuce cups for wrapping and scooping and lime wedges for garnish.

CAULIFLOWER TABOULI

Cauliflower is a surprisingly chameleon-like vegetable. I find myself using it in everything—frozen cauliflower in smoothies, pureed cauliflower in desserts, and now, grated cauliflower to mimic bulgar. Cauliflower absorbs the seasonings well, and the taste is fresh and vibrant. Absolutely loaded with nutrients, cauliflower contains potassium and phosphorous, which help support and repair the body's nervous system and immune system, muscles and bones. The ground sumac used in this recipe is a versatile spice with a tangy, lemony flavor, widely used in Middle Eastern recipes. It is available in Middle Eastern markets and the spice aisle of most grocery stores.

SERVES 6 TO 8

1 medium or 2 small heads of cauliflower

½ teaspoon pink salt, plus a good pinch

4 diced tomatoes

Seeds from 1 pomegranate

2 radishes, sliced thin

2 green onions, sliced thin

½ cup chopped fresh mint

½ cup chopped fresh parsley

3 tablespoons extra-virgin olive oil

2 tablespoons freshly squeezed lemon juice

2 tablespoons chopped pistachios

1 tablespoon lemon zest

½ teaspoon ground sumac

Good pinch of freshly ground black pepper

Combine the cauliflower and salt in a food processor and pulse until the cauliflower reaches a couscous-like consistency. Transfer the cauliflower to a nut milk bag or sieve, and gently press or squeeze to remove excess moisture. Transfer the cauliflower to a large bowl and add the tomatoes, pomegranate seeds, radishes, green onions, mint, parsley, olive oil, lemon juice, pistachios, lemon zest, sumac, and a good pinch of salt and black pepper. Toss well and serve immediately.

BEET HUMMUS

Hummus is one of those simple, perfect dishes that everyone loves. Spike it with beet for extra color and collagen-building vitamin C.

MAKES 2 CUPS

2 cups sprouted chickpeas (see page 31)

¾ cup water

½ beet, chopped

⅓ cup freshly squeezed lemon juice

¼ cup tahini

¼ cup extra-virgin olive oil

2 garlic cloves

2 tablespoons chopped fresh parsley

1 teaspoon ground cumin

1 teaspoon pink salt

Place all the ingredients in a food processor or blender and blend until smooth and creamy. Taste, and adjust seasonings if needed. Stored in an airtight container in the refrigerator, beet hummus will keep for up to 1 week.

FALAFELS

These bean-free falafels are made of seeds and spinach for a skin-repairing kick of iron and antioxidants, such as vitamins A and C.

MAKES 30

Dehydrator (optional)

1 cup pumpkin seeds, soaked
(see page 50)

½ cup sunflower seeds, soaked

¼ cup sesame seeds, soaked

1 cup chopped spinach

½ cup loosely packed fresh mint leaves

½ cup fresh cilantro leaves

1 garlic clove

2 tablespoons flaxseeds

2 tablespoons freshly squeezed lemon juice

2 tablespoons extra-virgin olive oil

2 tablespoons tahini

2 teaspoons apple cider vinegar

1 teaspoon ground cumin

1 teaspoon pink salt

Combine the pumpkin, sunflower, and sesame seeds in a food processor and process until they reach a couscous-like consistency. Transfer to a bowl and set aside.

Without cleaning the food processor, add the spinach, mint, cilantro, and garlic, and process until well chopped. Return the seed mixture to the food processor. Add the flaxseeds, lemon juice, olive oil, tahini, cider vinegar, cumin, and salt, and pulse until combined. (Be careful not to overprocess: you want a coarse texture, not a paste.)

Roll the mixture into about 30 balls and place on an unlined dehydrator tray. (**Tip:** Use wet hands for easier rolling.) Dehydrate the falafels for 6 hours, or until crispy on the outside but still moist inside (see page 59). Alternatively, you can bake the falafels in a 350°F preheated oven for 20 minutes, or until golden but still moist inside.

These falafels can be stored in an airtight container for up to 1 week in the refrigerator or 3 months in the freezer.

MINT TZATZIKI

A refreshing twist on traditional tzatziki. This one has a cashew sour cream base instead of dairy yogurt, and it is full of inflammation-taming, digestion-boosting mint.

MAKES 2 CUPS

Cashew Sour Cream (recipe follows)

½ cup loosely packed fresh mint leaves

½ cup grated cucumber

1 tablespoon chopped dill

Combine the sour cream and mint leaves in a blender and blend on high speed until incorporated. Transfer the mixture to a medium bowl. Remove excess moisture from the cucumber by squeezing out the grated pieces in handfuls. Then, fold in the cucumber and dill. Store in an airtight jar for up to 1 week in the refrigerator.

CASHEW SOUR CREAM

This sour cream is so addictive, you'll eat it by the spoonful. And the best thing? It's actually good for you.

MAKES 1½ CUPS

1 cup cashews, soaked (see page 50)

¼ cup water

Juice of 2 limes

1 Medjool date, pitted, or
1 teaspoon sweetener of choice

1 teaspoon extra-virgin olive oil

½ teaspoon pink salt

Combine all the ingredients in a blender and blend on high speed until smooth and creamy. Carefully add more water if needed to achieve the desired consistency. Transfer to an airtight glass jar and store in the refrigerator for up to 2 weeks.

RED PEPPER HUMMUS

A nut- and bean-free hummus! Made of vegetables and seeds, with some extra essentials like olive oil and tahini, this hummus is filled to the brim with lycopene, a nutrient that helps protect against the damage and aging to the skin caused by ultraviolet light, and reduces inflammation and stimulates cell renewal as well.

MAKES 3 CUPS

2 cups chopped zucchini

1 cup sunflower seeds, soaked (see page 50)

½ red bell pepper, chopped

¼ cup sun-dried tomatoes, soaked

¼ cup tahini

3 tablespoons freshly squeezed lemon juice

2 tablespoons extra-virgin olive oil

2 garlic cloves

1 tablespoon smoked paprika

1 teaspoon ground cumin

1 teaspoon pink salt

Combine all the ingredients in a blender and blend on high speed until smooth and creamy. Stored in an airtight container in the refrigerator, red pepper hummus will keep for up to 5 days.

FETTUCCINE ALFREDO

Entirely vegan, this healthy version of one my favorite indulgent dishes is a mainstay in our house. Unlike traditional Fettuccine Alfredo, my take is filled with nutritious ingredients, such as miso, cashews, turmeric, and zucchini. It is a great way to feel like you are indulging without any guilt.

SERVES 4 TO 6

Spiralizer (optional)

MARINATED MUSHROOMS

2½ cups wild mushrooms, sliced

3 tablespoons extra-virgin olive oil

2 tablespoons Bragg Liquid Aminos or tamari

2 garlic cloves, minced

1 teaspoon apple cider vinegar

2 sprigs of fresh thyme, crushed

ALFREDO SAUCE

1½ cups cashews, soaked (see page 50)

⅔ to 1 cup water

½ cup pine nuts or more cashews, soaked

¼ cup freshly squeezed lemon juice

2 tablespoons extra-virgin olive oil

2 tablespoons nutritional yeast

1 tablespoon white miso

1 garlic clove

1 teaspoon pink salt

½ teaspoon ground turmeric

¼ cup finely chopped fresh parsley

FETTUCCINE

4 zucchini

GARNISHES

Chopped parsley

Paprika

Freshly ground black pepper

To marinate the mushrooms, place all the ingredients in a large bowl and toss to coat. Allow to marinate for at least 30 minutes. The longer, the better. The mushrooms can be prepared a day in advance and stored in an airtight container in the refrigerator. Strain before using.

To make the sauce, combine the cashews, ⅔ cup of the water, pine nuts, lemon juice, olive oil, nutritional yeast, miso, garlic, salt, and turmeric in a blender and blend on high speed until smooth and creamy, the sauce should be thick but pourable. Add more water as necessary to achieve the desired consistency. Fold in the parsley and set aside.

(Continued)

To make the zucchini fettuccine, use a vegetable peeler to peel a zucchini and discard the skin. Continue to peel the flesh of the zucchini, turning it to create long, delicate fettuccine noodles. Alternatively, you can use a spiralizer. Repeat with the remaining zucchinis. Place the noodles in a large bowl and add the strained marinated mushrooms. Toss to coat.

To serve, divide the fettuccini and mushrooms among four to six bowls, spoon Alfredo sauce over the noodles and garnish with extra chopped parsley, pinches of paprika, and freshly ground black pepper.

CANNELLONI

This beautiful dish is as nutritious as it is satisfying. The added bonus is that it is quick to make. The walnuts in the filling transform this familiar dish into a nutrient-dense source of omega-3 fatty acids, which are essential for soft and plump skin.

SERVES 4

FILLING

2 cups walnuts, soaked (see page 50)

½ cup sun-dried tomatoes, soaked

½ carrot, grated

½ celery stalk, minced

1 shallot, minced

1 Medjool date, pitted

2 tablespoons Bragg Liquid Aminos or tamari

1 tablespoon fresh rosemary, finely minced

1 tablespoon extra-virgin olive oil

1 tablespoon balsamic vinegar

1 garlic clove

½ teaspoon lemon zest

½ teaspoon pink salt

Pinch of freshly grated nutmeg

CANNELLONI

2 zucchinis

1 tablespoon extra-virgin olive oil

½ teaspoon pink salt

TO SERVE

Tomato Sauce (recipe follows)

Chopped fresh herbs (such as basil, oregano, or marjoram)

Freshly ground black pepper

To make the filling, combine all the ingredients in a food processor and pulse until minced. Set aside.

To make the cannelloni shells, use a mandoline to thinly slice the zucchinis lengthways into long, pliable slices. Brush the slices with olive oil and sprinkle lightly with salt. Arrange one-quarter of the slices on a cutting board, side by side, with the long edges overlapping slightly, to create one large sheet. The short ends should be facing you.

Spoon one quarter of the filling along the bottom of the zucchini sheet. Roll the bottom edge of the sheet over the filling to enclose it, then continue rolling away from you until you reach the top edge. With the seam side down, slice the roll into 3 shorter rolls. Brush a little more olive oil on top of the cannelloni and set aside while you repeat the process with the remaining ingredients.

To serve, divide the tomato sauce evenly among four plates. Top with three stuffed cannellonis and garnish with fresh herbs and black pepper.

(Continued)

TOMATO SAUCE

MAKES ABOUT 3 CUPS

2 cups tomatoes, chopped

½ cup sundried tomatoes, soaked for 10 minutes

½ cup fresh basil leaves

Juice of 1 lemon

2 tablespoons minced red onion

2 Medjool dates, pitted

1 tablespoon fresh oregano

1 tablespoon olive oil

1 garlic clove

Put all the ingredients in a food processor and process until incorporated into a thick sauce.

SAVORY TARTS TWO WAYS

There's a natural versatility to tarts. You can (and should) choose your vegetables according to season to showcase the bright flavors and light textures of what's available. The possibilities are endless, which leaves the window wide open for creative combinations.

You can serve a pile of lightly dressed greens alongside these tarts and you've got a meal, then cut off a sliver a few hours later for a perfectly acceptable snack.

TART SHELLS

MAKES 4 SMALL TARTS
OR I LARGE TART

Dehydrator

¾ cup water

½ carrot, grated

¼ cup extra-virgin olive oil

½ shallot

1 garlic clove

2 cups almonds, soaked (see page 50)

1 cup macadamia nuts, soaked (see page 50)

2 tablespoons nutritional yeast

¾ cup flaxseeds, soaked, finely ground in a blender

2 teaspoons pink salt

1 tablespoon fresh thyme leaves

2 teaspoons fresh rosemary leaves

Pinch of freshly ground black pepper

Combine the water, carrot, olive oil, shallot, and garlic in a blender and blend on high speed until it reaches a smoothie-like consistency. Set aside.

Combine the almonds, macadamias, nutritional yeast, flaxseeds, salt, thyme, and rosemary in a food processor and pulse until the mixture resembles fine crumbs. Add the blended carrot mixture and black pepper and pulse until incorporated. Transfer the mixture to a large bowl and knead by hand until you have a workable dough. Mold the dough into either 4 tartlet shells about 3½ inches in diameter or 1 big one. Dehydrate at 118°F for 12 hours.

BASIL TOMATO TART
(SUMMER)

SERVES 4

3 cups Basic Nut Cheese
(page 175)

2 tablespoons chopped fresh basil

Freshly ground black pepper

Tart Shells (page 213)

2 cups Caramelized Tomatoes
(page 194)

Handful of microherbs (such as basil,
amaranth, or arugula), for garnish

Put the cheese, basil, and black pepper into a large bowl and stir to incorporate. Fill the tart shells with the cheese mixture and top with the caramelized tomatoes. Garnish with microherbs.

CARAMELIZED ONION & MUSHROOM TART
(WINTER)

SERVES 4

Dehydrator

2 cups thinly sliced red onions

1 cup small mushrooms of choice

¼ cup Bragg Liquid Aminos or tamari

¼ cup extra-virgin olive oil

2 tablespoons coconut nectar or maple syrup

2 sprigs of fresh thyme

½ teaspoon pink salt

Pinch of freshly ground black pepper

Tart Shells (page 213)

4 cups Herb & Flower Nut Cheese (page 178)

½ cup chopped fresh herbs (such as basil, thyme, amaranth, or arugula) or microgreens, for garnish

Line 2 dehydrator trays with nonstick baking sheets. In a large bowl, combine the onions, mushrooms, Liquid Aminos, olive oil, coconut nectar, thyme, salt, and black pepper, and toss to coat. Spread the vegetables on the prepared dehydrator trays and drizzle with any marinade remaining in the bowl. Dehydrate for 5 hours, flip the vegetables with a spatula, and dehydrate for 5 hours more, or until caramelized (see page 59).

Fill the tart shells with the herb and flower nut cheese and top with the caramelized vegetables. Garnish with the fresh herbs or microgreens. Serve at room temperature, or heat the tarts in the dehydrator for a few minutes first.

CHICKPEA PANCAKES
WITH BEET RAITA & CARROT CUMIN SALAD

These pancakes are totally delicious and have the huge advantage of being made with just a few ingredients. Not only is chickpea flour easy to work with, it is gluten free and high in fiber and protein. These pancakes are also incredibly versatile—I like to fold them over fillings to make delicious sandwiches. If you don't have chickpea flour in your cupboard, you can easily make it using fully dried sprouted chickpeas: just pop them into a blender and pulverize on high speed until the chickpeas are broken down into a fine powder and a flour begins to form.

SERVES 4

BEET RAITA

¾ cup shredded beet

¼ cup finely diced shallot

1 garlic clove, finely minced

Juice of ½ lime

2 teaspoons pink salt

2 cups plain unsweetened coconut milk yogurt

2 tablespoons extra-virgin olive oil

2 tablespoons sliced fresh mint

1 tablespoon minced fresh cilantro

Freshly ground black pepper

CARROT CUMIN SALAD

2 carrots

2 tablespoons extra-virgin olive oil

2 tablespoons minced fresh cilantro

1 tablespoon freshly squeezed lemon juice

1 tablespoon fresh orange juice

1 tablespoon chia seeds

1 teaspoon cumin seeds

½ teaspoon pink salt

Freshly ground black pepper

PANCAKES

1 cup chickpea flour

½ cup fermented veggies of choice

½ cup water

1 teaspoon ground turmeric

½ teaspoon pink salt

2 tablespoons coconut oil

TO SERVE

2 cups watercress

2 cups sprouts

To make the beet raita, put the beet, shallot, garlic, lime juice, and salt into a medium bowl and toss to combine. Let sit for 10 minutes. Carefully pour off any liquid that has accumulated in the bowl. Add the coconut yogurt, olive oil, mint, and cilantro, and gently fold together. Add black pepper to taste and more salt if desired.

To make the carrot cumin salad, cut the carrots into long, thin strips using a vegetable peeler or sharp knife. Place the carrot strips into a medium bowl. Add the olive oil, cilantro, lemon juice, orange juice, chia seeds, cumin, and salt and gently fold together. Add black pepper to taste and more salt if desired.

To make the pancakes, combine the chickpea flour, fermented veggies, water, turmeric, and salt in a blender and blend on high speed until completely smooth. If the mixture is too thick, add a little water until the desired consistency is achieved. You can also cover the batter and leave it in the refrigerator overnight to ferment.

In a cast-iron skillet over medium-high heat, heat the coconut oil. Pour ¼ cup of the batter onto the hot skillet and spread thinly and evenly with the back of a spoon. Cook for around 3 minutes until it forms a crisp golden crust. Drizzle the skillet with a little more oil if needed and flip, cooking for a further 2 minutes, or until cooked through on the second side. Transfer the pancake to a plate and repeat the process until you have made 4 pancakes.

To serve, place a pancake on each plate and top with 2 tablespoons the beet raita, 2 tablespoons of the carrot cumin salad, and a handful each of watercress and sprouts.

GREEN QUINOA PILAF BOWL
WITH TURMERIC SAUCE

This vibrantly green bowl is full of fresh ingredients that vitalize and nourish, and it will uplift any weeknight lineup. Don't be deterred by the lengthy ingredient list: this recipe is incredibly easy to prepare and convenient—once you've tried it, you'll find yourself turning to it again and again. But the real reason to obsess over this green bowl? All the beauty and health benefits!

When it comes to balancing your pH levels, the more green food the better. When you balance your pH, your body becomes an inhospitable environment for disease. Having a more alkaline body is fundamental to a calm and joyful life and also brings an overall glow, with radiant skin and sparkling eyes.

SERVES 4

Dehydrator

DEHYDRATED VEGETABLES

2 cups broccoli florets

2 cups asparagus cut into
2-inch lengths, tough ends removed

2 tablespoons olive oil

Pinch of pink salt

TURMERIC SAUCE

1 cup sunflower seeds, soaked
(see page 50)

½ cup fresh orange juice

¼ cup extra-virgin olive oil

2 Medjool dates, pitted

2 garlic cloves, crushed

2 tablespoons freshly squeezed
lemon juice

1 tablespoon apple cider vinegar

½ teaspoon pink salt

1 teaspoon smoked paprika

1 teaspoon ground turmeric

½ teaspoon ground chipotle

QUINOA PILAF

2 cups cooked quinoa

2 tablespoons extra-virgin olive oil

1 garlic clove, minced

½ cup green onions, minced

2 tablespoons minced fresh parsley

2 tablespoons chopped fresh basil

1 tablespoon freshly squeezed lemon
juice

Pink salt

Freshly ground black pepper

TO SERVE

2 cups arugula

2 avocados, diced

2 tablespoons pumpkin seeds

Seeds from 1 pomegranate

221

To make the dehydrated vegetables, line a dehydrator tray with a nonstick baking sheet. Put the broccoli and asparagus into a big bowl and drizzle with the olive oil and sprinkle with the salt. Toss well to coat. Distribute the vegetables over the prepared dehydrator tray and dehydrate for 1 hour (see page 59). Alternatively, you could omit the olive oil and salt and blanch the broccoli and asparagus in boiling water.

For the sauce, combine all the ingredients in a blender and blend on high speed until smooth and creamy. The sauce should be pourable but not runny. Add a little water if necessary to achieve the desired consistency.

To make the pilaf, put the quinoa, olive oil, garlic, green onions, parsley, basil, and lemon juice into a large bowl and toss well to coat. Season with salt and black pepper to taste.

To serve, divide the pilaf among four bowls. Top with the dehydrated vegetables, arugula, and avocados. Dollop a generous spoonful of the turmeric sauce on top of each bowl and sprinkle with pumpkin seeds and pomegranate.

MOROCCAN SPICED BOWL
WITH RAINBOW QUINOA

Use some classic Moroccan spices like cumin and cinnamon to turn your autumn bowl into an unforgettably chic main course. If you're looking for an excuse to eat more seasonal vegetables, you've found just the recipe that will help you devour tons of beautifying veggies in a delicious and hearty way for colder weather.

SERVES 4

2 cups cooked quinoa

Juice of 1 lemon

1 tablespoon extra-virgin olive oil

1 teaspoon ground turmeric

1 teaspoon ground cumin

1 teaspoon ground ginger, or
1 tablespoon fresh ginger juice

1 teaspoon smoked paprika

½ teaspoon ground cinnamon

½ teaspoon ground cardamom

2 cups finely sliced seasonal vegetables
(such as fennel, zucchini, celery, green
onions, and red or yellow bell peppers)

1 orange, cut into segments

½ cup minced fresh mint

2 tablespoons chopped fresh cilantro

½ fresh red chili pepper, sliced

Pink salt

Freshly ground black pepper

1 cup Moroccan Spiced Pumpkin Salad
with Chickpea Popcorn (page 154)

2 tablespoons plain unsweetened
coconut milk yogurt

Seeds from 1 pomegranate, for garnish

Put the quinoa, lemon juice, olive oil, turmeric, cumin, ginger, paprika, cinnamon, and cardamom into a large bowl and fluff with a fork to combine. Add the seasonal vegetables, orange, mint, cilantro, and chili pepper, and toss to combine. Season with salt and black pepper to taste.

To serve, divide the quinoa salad among four bowls and top with spiced pumpkin salad and chickpeas. Top each bowl with a small dollop of coconut yogurt and garnish with pomegranate seeds.

DESSERTS

I have such a sweet tooth, and making desserts is one of my very favorite ways to spend time. I particularly love challenging myself to create new, healthier versions of decadent favorites such as Tiramisu Cups (page 235), Matcha Raw-eos (page 245), and Coffee Rose Chocolate (page 252).

All of these dessert recipes are free of refined sugars, gluten, and empty fillers, and full of flavor and ingredients that love you back. They also happen to be entirely made from plants. There's nothing like indulging in rich desserts and eating yourself beautiful in the process.

MOCHA MOUSSE TART
WITH CARAMEL FILLING

This velvety chocolate cream tart has a gooey caramel filling. Amazingly enough, this irresistible, rich dessert is dairy free!

SERVES 6 TO 8

TART SHELL

2 cups almonds, soaked, reserve soaking liquid (see page 50)

2 cups gluten-free oats

2 cups Medjool dates, pitted

½ cup almond butter

¼ cup maple syrup

2 tablespoons cacao powder

1 tablespoon maca powder (optional)

1 teaspoon vanilla bean powder

1 teaspoon pink salt

CARAMEL FILLING

8 Medjool dates, pitted

1 cup unsalted peanut butter or almond butter

¼ cup coconut oil, melted

¼ cup raw honey or coconut nectar

1 teaspoon vanilla bean powder

1 teaspoon pink salt

MOCHA MOUSSE

3 avocados

¾ cup unsweetened coconut milk or plant milk of choice

½ cup cacao powder

2 tablespoons raw honey or maple syrup, or 8 Medjool dates, pitted

1 to 2 teaspoons ground espresso powder, according to preference

1 teaspoon vanilla bean powder

Pinch of pink salt

To make the tart shell, put the almonds and oats into a food processor and process until they reach the consistency of fine breadcrumbs. Add the dates, almond butter, maple syrup, cacao powder, maca powder, if using, vanilla powder, and salt, and process until the mixture forms a sticky dough. Cover the dough with plastic wrap and refrigerate for about 30 minutes, until firm.

Press the dough into the bottom and sides of a tart pan and refrigerate until needed.

To make the caramel filling, combine all the ingredients in a blender and blend on high speed until completely smooth, adding some of the reserved soaking liquid if needed. Spread the filling evenly over the bottom of the tart shell and return it to the refrigerator while you make the mousse.

To make the mousse, combine all the ingredients in a blender and blend on high speed until smooth and creamy. Spread the mousse over the caramel filling in an attractive pattern using the back of a spoon. Refrigerate until set, about 2 hours. Cut into slices and serve.

MATCHA LIME MOUSSE

This exquisite dessert is a snap to make. Velvety avocado mousse spiked with matcha and lime give this sweet treat an anti-inflammatory and immunity-enhancing boost. The result is a powerful, tangy, spoonable dessert that's perfect for a healthy and supercharged pick-me-up.

SERVES 6

2 cups avocado flesh

1 cup cashews, soaked (see page 50)

½ cup coconut nectar or sweetener of choice

½ cup unsweetened coconut milk or plant milk of choice

1 tablespoon freshly squeezed lime juice

2 teaspoons matcha

½ teaspoon spirulina

Pinch of pink salt

½ cup coconut oil, melted

Zest of ½ lime, for garnish

To prepare the mousse, combine the avocado, cashews, sweetener, coconut milk, lime juice, matcha, spirulina, and salt in a blender and blend on high speed until smooth and creamy. Add the melted coconut oil and blend to combine. Pour the mousse into cups and refrigerate for at least 2 hours to set. Garnish with lime zest and serve.

PASSION FRUIT TART

This light, refreshing tart is a flavor explosion. Loads of tangy passion fruit paired with a lime and ginger crust make the perfect contrast in textures and flavors. Rich in vitamins C and A, these fruits are also excellent for hydrated glowing skin. This tart is a great dessert for company—I usually whip one up when I need something impressive and I'm short on time.

SERVES 8

TART SHELL

2 cups macadamia nuts, soaked (see page 50)

½ cup unsweetened shredded coconut

1 cup Medjool dates, pitted

2 tablespoons coconut oil, melted, plus more for greasing pan

2 teaspoons lime zest

1 teaspoon grated ginger

½ teaspoon pink salt

FILLING

Pulp from 8 to 10 passion fruits (to yield about ½ cup of strained juice)

2 cups cashews, soaked (see page 50)

½ cup coconut cream

¼ cup maple syrup

2 tablespoons freshly squeezed lime juice

1 teaspoon vanilla bean powder

½ teaspoon pink salt

⅓ cup coconut oil, melted

GARNISH

Pulp from 2 passion fruits

To make the tart shell, first use coconut oil to grease a 9-inch tart pan with a removable bottom. Combine the macadamias and coconut in a food processor and pulse until they form coarse crumbs. Add the dates, coconut oil, lime zest, ginger, and salt and pulse until combined. Press the dough evenly and firmly into the bottom and sides of the tart pan. Refrigerate until needed.

To make the filling, put the passion fruit pulp into a blender and pulse a couple of times to separate the seeds from the pulp. Strain the mixture through a sieve placed over a bowl. Discard the seeds.

Return the passion fruit juice to the blender and add the cashews, coconut cream, maple syrup, lime juice, vanilla powder, and salt. Blend on high speed until smooth and creamy. Add the coconut oil and blend until combined. Pour the filling into the chilled tart shell and refrigerate for 2 hours, or until set. When ready to serve, decorate the top of the tart with passion fruit pulp.

TIRAMISU CUPS

Tiramisu is my favorite dessert of all time. When I received my first paycheck as a chef, I celebrated by having the most delicious tiramisu at a local restaurant. It was so wonderful that I would often go there just for that amazing treat. Over the years, I have tried to create a healthy version, but it was only recently that I landed on the right combination of flavors and textures. Making the sponge out of creamy macadamia nuts and gluten-free oats is such a delicious alternative. Cacao butter gives the perfect velvety texture to the ganache and vanilla cream.

MAKES 8 CUPS

COFFEE CAKE

2 cups macadamia nuts, soaked (see page 50)

2 tablespoons gluten-free oats

1 tablespoon cacao powder

½ teaspoon pink salt

1 cup Medjool dates, pitted

½ cup Spiced Cold Brew (page 79)

VANILLA CREAM

1 cup cashews, soaked (see page 50)

½ cup coconut cream

¼ cup cacao butter, melted

¼ cup sweetener

1 teaspoon vanilla bean powder

Juice of ½ lemon

½ teaspoon pink salt

CHOCOLATE GANACHE

¼ cup cacao butter, melted

¼ cup coconut oil, melted

2 tablespoons maple syrup or sweetener of choice

½ cup cacao powder

1 teaspoon vanilla bean powder

Pinch of pink salt

GARNISH

Cacao powder

To make the coffee cake, combine the macadamias, oats, cacao powder, and salt in a food processor and process until finely ground. Add the dates and brewed coffee and process until the mixture resembles runny, grainy cake dough. Set aside.

To make the vanilla cream, combine all the ingredients in a blender and blend on high speed until smooth and creamy. Set aside.

To make the chocolate ganache, whisk together the melted cacao butter and coconut oil and the maple syrup in a medium bowl. Add the cacao powder, vanilla powder, and salt, and whisk until everything is well combined and a shiny sauce forms.

To assemble the tiramisu, place 1 tablespoon of the coffee cake into each of eight serving cups and gently spread out in an even layer with the back of a spoon. Set aside the remaining coffee cake. Add vanilla cream until each cup is halfway full. Top with a layer of ganache. Place the cups in the freezer to chill for 30 minutes, or until starting to set. Remove the cups from the freezer, delicately add more coffee cake, and use the back of your spoon to lightly even out the surface, taking care not to apply any pressure. Cover with half of the remaining vanilla cream, followed by the chocolate ganache. Transfer to the freezer to chill for about 30 minutes, until the new layers are set. Add a final layer of the remaining vanilla cream and refrigerate overnight. Dust with some cacao powder before serving.

BLUEBERRY ACAI CRUMBLE

My grandmother made the most amazing warm apple crumble. This recipe is inspired by her original recipe, but I wanted to add some of my favorite superfoods to create a version that is both comforting and full of amazing ingredients. Blueberries provide just the right amount of tartness and oats give this a creamy, comforting texture. Because I`m a superfood addict, and one can never get enough of beauty-enhancing acai, I added a little for good measure.

SERVES 8

CRUST

1 cup macadamia nuts, soaked and then dried (see page 50)

1 cup rolled oats

2 tablespoons maple syrup

1 tablespoon coconut oil, melted, plus more for greasing pan

1 teaspoon ground ginger

1 teaspoon ground cardamom

½ teaspoon vanilla bean powder

FILLING

2 cups blueberries

4 Medjool dates, pitted

2 tablespoons maple syrup

1 tablespoon acai powder

1 tablespoon coconut oil, melted

1 tablespoon freshly squeezed lemon juice

½ teaspoon ground cardamom

½ teaspoon vanilla powder

¼ cup chia seeds

CRUMBLE TOPPING

1 cup almond flour

½ cup rolled oats

2 tablespoons chopped crystallized ginger, or 1 teaspoon ground ginger

1 teaspoon ground cardamom

1 teaspoon pink salt

½ teaspoon vanilla bean powder

2 tablespoons maple syrup

1 tablespoon coconut oil, melted

Line a rectangular baking pan with parchment paper and grease with coconut oil. To make the base, combine the macadamia nuts and oats in a food processor and process into a flour. Add the maple syrup, coconut oil, ginger, cardamom, and vanilla powder, and pulse until well combined. Press the dough into the bottom of the prepared pan. Refrigerate until needed.

To make the filling, combine the blueberries, dates, maple syrup, acai powder, coconut oil, lemon juice, cardamom, and vanilla powder in a blender and blend on high speed until almost smooth but not quite. Add the chia seeds and pulse to combine. Let the mixture stand for 5 minutes, or until it starts to thicken slightly. Pour the mixture over the base. Return the pan to the fridge to chill while you make the crumble.

To make the crumble topping, stir together the almond flour, oats, ginger, cardamom, salt, and vanilla powder in a large bowl. Add the maple syrup and coconut oil, and work them in with your fingertips just until incorporated. Crumble the topping mixture over the acai filling and press down lightly to adhere. Refrigerate the finished crumble for 1 hour, or until set, or heat it up in the dehydrator or oven and eat it by the spoonful.

WHITE CHOCOLATE GINGER RASPBERRY CAKE
WITH BROWNIE CRUST

It's hard to explain how recipes come about. Sometimes it's a combination of flavors that one can nearly taste, and other times it's an aesthetic vision of colors, layers, and ingredients that will look perfect together. This recipe was a mixture of both, bursting with flavor and beautiful to look at.

SERVES 8

BROWNIE CRUST

1 cup almonds, soaked (see page 50)

½ cup cashews, soaked (see page 50)

½ cup maple syrup, or 1 cup Medjool dates, pitted

2 tablespoons cacao powder

2 tablespoons cacao nibs

½ teaspoon vanilla bean powder

¼ cup cacao butter, melted

GINGER FILLING

1½ cups cashews, soaked (see page 50)

½ cup unsweetened coconut milk or plant milk of choice

½ cup coconut butter

⅓ cup maple syrup or coconut nectar

2 tablespoons grated fresh ginger

1 tablespoon lucuma powder

Juice of 1 lime

1 teaspoon lime zest

1 teaspoon vanilla bean powder

RASPBERRY TOPPING

1 pint raspberries fresh or frozen

Line a rectangular baking pan with parchment paper or plastic wrap. To make the brownie crust, combine the almonds, cashews, maple syrup, cacao powder, cacao nibs, and vanilla powder in a food processor and process until thoroughly combined—it should have a sticky texture. Add the cacao butter and pulse until the mixture forms a dough. Transfer the brownie mixture into the prepared pan and press it evenly into the bottom of the pan. Refrigerate until needed.

To make the ginger filling, combine all the ingredients in a blender and blend on high speed until very smooth and creamy. Pour over the brownie base. Top with the raspberries, pressing lightly so they are half submerged in the ginger mixture. Refrigerate for 1 hour, or until set.

MACADAMIA SHORTBREAD & SALTED CARAMEL BARS

These delicious bars have a macadamia shortbread-cookie layer topped with salted date caramel, all of which is coated in a thin layer of chocolate. I can never resist these, and have even been known to have a stack hidden at the bottom of my freezer. For those days when I need something sweet fast, I defrost one for 10 minutes before eating, and it is perfect.

MAKES 12

MACADAMIA SHORTBREAD

1 cup macadamia nuts, soaked (see page 50)

¾ cup unsweetened shredded coconut

3 tablespoons maple syrup or sweetener of choice

1 tablespoon coconut oil, melted, plus more if needed

½ teaspoon vanilla bean powder

½ teaspoon pink salt

SALTED CARAMEL LAYER

10 Medjool dates, pitted

2 tablespoons unsalted peanut or cashew butter

2 tablespoons unsweetened coconut milk or plant milk of choice

2 tablespoons coconut oil, melted

1 teaspoon pink salt

CHOCOLATE COATING

⅓ cup cacao butter, melted

3 tablespoons cacao powder

2 tablespoons maple syrup

1 tablespoon coconut oil, melted

½ teaspoon vanilla bean powder

Pinch of pink salt

Line a loaf pan with parchment paper. To make the shortbread, combine the macadamias and coconut in a food processor and process until they form fine crumbs. Add the maple syrup, coconut oil, vanilla powder, and salt, and process until they come together into a dough. It should be crumbly and moist and hold its shape when pressed between two fingers. If the mixture is too crumbly, add a bit more melted coconut oil. Transfer the dough into the prepared loaf pan and press into the bottom of the pan. Place in the freezer to chill while you make the caramel.

To make the caramel, combine all the ingredients in a blender and blend on high speed until smooth. Add a little water if needed to form a thick caramel. Spread the caramel evenly over the cookie layer. Return to the freezer to chill for 3 hours, or until solid.

To make the chocolate coating, whisk all the ingredients in a small bowl until smooth and shiny. Set aside.

Remove the pan from the freezer and lay a piece of parchment paper on your work surface. With a sharp knife, cut the caramel-covered shortbread into bars of whatever size you prefer. One at a time, dip each bar into the chocolate turning to coat all sides, and place on the parchment paper. Refrigerate for 1 hour, or until set.

MATCHA RAW-EOS

These raw, healthy sandwich cookies never fails to impress people. A pair of delicious chocolate cookies sandwiching a dreamy cream filling that is actually good for you? Yes, please! As a matcha lover, I just had to add a bit to the filling to turn these cookies into a skin-nourishing treat.

**MAKES 12 SMALL
SANDWICH COOKIES**

COOKIES

1 cup macadamia nuts, soaked and then dried (see page 50)

½ cup gluten-free oats

¼ cup flaxseeds

½ cup Medjool dates, pitted

¼ cup cacao powder

1 tablespoon cacao butter, melted

½ teaspoon vanilla bean powder

Pinch of pink salt

MATCHA FILLING

1 cup cashews, soaked

2 tablespoons coconut oil, melted

2 tablespoons maple syrup

2 teaspoons matcha

½ teaspoon vanilla bean powder

To make the cookies, combine the macadamias, oats, and flaxseeds in a food processor and process into a flour. Add the dates, cacao powder, cacao butter, vanilla powder, and salt, and process until the mixture forms a dough. Refrigerate for 10 minutes, or until firm.

Place the dough in between two pieces of parchment paper and roll it out to the desired thickness. Cut out circles with a cookie cutter and arrange the cookies on a baking sheet. Place in the freezer to chill while you make the filling.

To make the filling, combine all the ingredients in a blender and blend on high speed until smooth and creamy. Spread filling on top of half of the chilled cookies and sandwich together with the remaining cookies. Stored in an airtight container in the refrigerator, these cookies will keep for up to 1 week.

DOUGHNUTS

With doughnut mania going around, and so many amazing new flavors popping up, I had to have a go at making a (healthy) version or two of my own. The addition of superfoods is a perfect way to boost the benefits of these addictive little jewels. You may opt to dehydrate them so they become more cake-like.

CHOCOLATE MACA DOUGHNUTS

MAKES 12 DOUGHNUTS

DOUGHNUTS

2 cups macadamia nuts, soaked and dried (see page 50)

1 cup almonds, soaked and dried

¾ cup Medjool dates

½ cup cashew or almond butter

¼ cup cacao powder

¼ cup coconut oil, melted

1 tablespoon maca powder

½ teaspoon vanilla bean powder

½ teaspoon pink salt

¼ teaspoon ground cinnamon

CHOCOLATE FROSTING

½ cup cacao powder

¼ cup cacao butter, melted

2 tablespoons coconut oil, melted

2 tablespoons maple syrup

½ teaspoon vanilla bean powder

Pinch of pink salt

GARNISH

Dried rose petals

To make the doughnuts, combine the macadamias and almonds in a food processor and process into a flour. Add the dates, cashew butter, cacao powder, coconut oil, maca powder, vanilla powder, salt, and cinnamon, and process until the mixture forms a dough that holds together well. Divide the dough into 12 equal pieces.

Line a baking sheet with parchment paper. Soften the dough with your hands and roll it into a ½-inch-thick rope about 24 inches long. Pinch off a 2-inch piece and wrap the ends together to form a ring and place it on the prepared baking sheet. Repeat to make 12 donuts. Alternatively, press the dough into silicone doughnut molds. Place in the freezer to chill while you make the frosting.

To make the frosting, combine all the ingredients in a blender and blend on high speed until smooth and creamy. Drizzle the chocolate over the doughnuts, garnish with rose petals, and serve.

PINK DOUGHNUTS
WITH STRAWBERRY ACAI FROSTING

MAKES 12 DOUGHNUTS

DOUGHNUTS

2 cups macadamia nuts, soaked and dried (see page 50)

1 cup almonds, soaked and dried

¾ cup Medjool dates

½ cup cashew or macadamia butter

¼ cup coconut oil, melted

3 tablespoons grated beet

2 tablespoons lucuma powder

1 teaspoon vanilla bean powder

½ teaspoon pink salt

STRAWBERRY FROSTING

1 cup cashews, soaked (see page 50)

¼ cup chopped strawberries

¼ cup cacao butter, melted

3 tablespoons raw honey or coconut nectar

2 tablespoons unsweetened coconut milk or plant milk of choice

1 tablespoon freshly squeezed lemon juice

1 teaspoon acai powder

½ teaspoon vanilla bean powder

GARNISH

Unsweetened coconut chips

To make the doughnuts combine the macadamias and almonds in a food processor and process into a flour. Add the dates, cashew butter, coconut oil, beet, lucuma powder, vanilla powder, and salt, and process until the mixture forms a dough that holds together well. Divide the dough into 12 equal pieces.

Line a baking sheet with parchment paper. Soften the dough with your hands and roll it into a ½-inch-thick rope about 24 inches long. Pinch off a 2-inch piece and wrap the ends together to form a ring and place it on the prepared baking sheet. Repeat to make 12 donuts. Alternatively, press the dough into silicone doughnut molds. Place in the freezer to chill while you make the frosting.

To make the frosting, place all the ingredients in a blender and blend on high speed until smooth and creamy. Drizzle the doughnuts with the frosting or pour the frosting into a small bowl and dip the doughnuts in. Garnish with coconut chips and serve.

BASIC CHOCOLATE RECIPE
WITH THREE VARIATIONS

There is something so wonderful about making chocolate at home. This version is easy and fast, and the results are always perfect. With few ingredients as a base, you can let your creativity run loose with spices, herbs, flowers, superfoods—you name it. You will impress everyone with your chocolate-making skills.

These variations are nearly too pretty to eat—but go ahead, have some! These chocolates have a delicate, magical taste—each bite is surprising and exciting.

MAKES ABOUT 2 CUPS

2 cups cacao butter

¼ cup raw honey, maple syrup, or coconut nectar

2 tablespoons coconut oil

¼ cup cacao powder

1 teaspoon vanilla bean powder

⅛ teaspoon pink salt

Line a shallow dish with parchment paper and set aside.

In the top of a double boiler over barely simmering water, melt the cacao butter, honey, and coconut oil, and stir until smooth. Remove the top of the double boiler from the heat and add the cacao powder, vanilla powder, and salt. Stir until the mixture has a velvety texture without clumps.

Pour the warm chocolate into the prepared dish or candy mold and refrigerate for an hour, or until firm. Break the chocolate into chunks and store in an airtight container at room temperature for up to 5 days or in the refrigerator for up to 1 month.

MATCHA CHOCOLATE

Follow the basic recipe, but replace the cacao powder with 2 teaspoons matcha and ½ teaspoon ground ginger. After pouring the chocolate into the dish or candy mold, decorate it with edible flowers and then place in the refrigerator.

WHITE CHOCOLATE CARDAMOM & RASPBERRIES

Follow the basic recipe, but replace the cacao powder with 1 teaspoon ground cardamom. After pouring the chocolate into the dish or candy mold, decorate it with fresh cut raspberries and then place in the refrigerator.

COFFEE ROSE CHOCOLATE

Follow the basic recipe, but along with the cacao powder also add 2 teaspoons finely ground espresso. After pouring the chocolate into the dish or candy mold, decorate it with dried rose petals and then place in the refrigerator.

VANILLA & SALTED CARAMEL ICE CREAM BARS
WITH A CHOCOLATE COATING

Ice cream is the quintessential summer treat. You can easily find inexpensive molds that will make these recipes super fun to create.

MAKES 12 ICE CREAM BARS

Ice-pop molds and sticks

VANILLA ICE CREAM

2 cups unsweetened coconut milk or plant milk of choice

¾ cup cashews, soaked (see page 50)

¼ cup coconut nectar or sweetener of choice

1 teaspoon vanilla bean powder

1 teaspoon mesquite powder

SALTED CARAMEL ICE CREAM

5 Medjool dates, pitted

2 tablespoons almond butter

1 tablespoon coconut nectar or sweetener of choice

1 teaspoon pink salt

½ teaspoon mesquite powder

CHOCOLATE COATING

¾ cup cacao powder

⅓ cup coconut oil, melted

⅓ cup cacao butter, melted

¼ cup maple syrup

½ teaspoon vanilla bean powder

GARNISH

½ cup slivered almonds

To make the vanilla ice cream, combine all the ingredients in a high-speed blender and blend until completely smooth. Pour the mixture into ice-pop molds, filling them up about two-thirds of the way. There will be some vanilla mixture left in the blender. Place the molds in the freezer to chill while you prepare the caramel.

To make the salted caramel ice cream, add all the ingredients to the remaining vanilla mixture and blend until completely smooth. Remove the molds from the freezer and pour the caramel mixture on top of the vanilla to fill the molds. Use a teaspoon to lightly swirl the two ice creams together. Insert the handles and return the pops to the freezer to freeze overnight, or until set.

Line a baking sheet with parchment paper. Once the ice cream has frozen, briefly run the molds under warm water to help release the ice cream bar from the molds and once they are out, place them on the prepared baking sheet. Put the baking sheet in the freezer to stay cold while you make the chocolate coating.

To make the chocolate coating, put the cacao powder into a medium heatproof bowl and place over a bowl of hot water. Add the coconut oil and cacao butter and stir until smooth and glossy. Add the maple syrup and vanilla bean powder, and stir until well combined. Pour the chocolate mixture into a tall, wide glass. One at a time, remove an ice cream bar from freezer and quickly dip it in the chocolate. Gently shake off the excess chocolate (so the chocolate coating won't be too thick) and immediately sprinkle the bar with the almonds to garnish. Return the bar to the freezer and repeat the process to coat the remaining bars. Freeze for at least 5 minutes, or until the chocolate on the last ice cream bars has set. These will keep in the freezer for up to 1 month.

COCONUT ROSE RASPBERRY ICE CREAM BARS

This combination is very delicate and whimsical. The raspberries lend an element of surprise when you bite into this deliciously creamy coconut creation. Infused with rose and cardamom, these ice cream bars will transport you to a Persian rose garden.

MAKES 12 ICE CREAM BARS

Ice-pop molds and sticks

1 cup unsweetened coconut milk

1 cup young Thai coconut meat

2 tablespoons coconut nectar or sweetener of choice

1 teaspoon rose water

1 teaspoon ground cardamom

½ teaspoon vanilla bean powder

1 pint raspberries

Combine the coconut milk, coconut meat, coconut nectar, rose water, cardamom, and vanilla powder in a blender and blend on high speed until smooth and creamy. Distribute the raspberries among the ice-pop molds. Pour the coconut mixture over the raspberries to fill the molds. Insert the handles. Freeze for 3 to 4 hours, until set. When ready to eat, briefly run the molds under warm water to help release the ice cream bars. These will keep in the freezer for up to 1 month.

ACKNOWLEDGMENTS

It takes a village . . . It's amazing to think just how many people have contributed to the making of this book over the past two years. And this is exactly how the birth of this book came to be—with the help and creativity of so many people. It might be offering a tweak in a recipe, opening the doors to an amazing kitchen for a photoshoot, bringing amazing organic produce to my doorstep for crafting, or looking after my children—all of these meaningful gestures have contributed to the collaborative effort that is this beautiful book.

These are just some of the people that have worked on it—by no means all—so a huge thank you to everyone mentioned and not mentioned here.

I have to thank my agent, Sharon Bowers, for taking a chance on me, believing in my work, and making it possible for this girl from Portugal to have one—of many books to come—published in the US.

To my editor, Juree Sondker, and Sara Bercholz at Roost Books for believing in my work and vision, and having the patience to work with me and around different time zones. To assistant editor Audra Figgins and the amazing team at Roost and Shambhala Publications for making my body of work into a beautiful book.

There are a couple of wonderful people that have been central to this project. To Ana Trancoso, on styling and props—she has an amazing eye and adds a positive "we can do anything" vibe to every situation! To Antonio Nascimento, on photography, for his patience, persistence, and extra days. To Quinta do Arneiro in Portugal for opening their doors for us to shoot in their amazing kitchen and field.

To my children, partner, and family, for sharing me with my other love: food.

And to all of you that are holding this book, thank you for supporting my dream of creating, crafting, and sharing plant-based food—this book is for you!

xx
Mafalda

RESOURCES

KITCHEN TOOLS

Dehydrator A dehydrator is a low-temperature oven about the size of a microwave that slowly removes the moisture from foods—cooking the ingredients while still maintaining their nutritional integrity. Here are two great options.

Excalibur Dehydrator || excaliburdehydrator.com
Sedona Dehydrator || tribestlife.com

Fermentation Crock

Sarah Kersten Ceramic Fermentation Crock || sarahkersten.com/collections/fermentation-jars

Food Processor I've had my food processor for over ten years, and it still works like a dream. I recommend this one!

Cuisinart Food Processor || cuisinart.com

Glass Straws A great reusable option for all those tasty smoothies, milks, and juices.

Glass Dharma || glassdharma.com

High-Speed Blender I recommend a Vitamix—the best, most high-powered option for a blender that will truly last a lifetime.

Vitamix || vitamix.com

Juicer I begin nearly every day with a fresh-pressed juice, so this is a great investment in your health and well-being. Here are two great options for juicers.

Omega || omegajuicers.com
Norwalk || norwalkjuicers.com

Knives Great kitchen knives are a must: if you have one good knife, you will be prepared for anything. Here is one of my favorite brands.

Global || globalcutleryusa.com

Mandoline To quickly slice veggies and fruits into thin slices and minimize prep time, you will love this handy tool.

Kyocera Adjustable Slicer || kyoceraadvancedceramics.com
Japanese Mandoline || whisknyc.com/japanese-mandoline

Nut Milk Bag Here is my favorite option for a washable, reusable nut milk bag.

Elaina Love Amazing Nut Milk Bag || store.purejoyplanet.com

Produce Bag Skip the plastic grocery bags and invest in a few reusable produce bags!

Organic Muslin Produce Bag || ecobags.com

Spiralizer For all your vegetable noodle needs, here are a few different spiralizers to give a whirl.

Gefu Handheld Spiralizer || gefu.com/en/kitchen-tools.html
Paderno Spiralizer || padernousa.com

ADAPTOGENS

Anima Mundi Apothecary This NYC-based company sources their botanicals from Central and South America, working with native peoples to support fair trade, permacultural outreach, the development of small economies, and plant-based remedies. || animamundiherbals.com

CAP Beauty Through the philosophy "Beauty is Wellness, Wellness is Beauty," CAP shares products, practices, and knowledge that teem with plant power and create change from the outside in. || capbeauty.com

Moon Juice Based in California, this is a great source for adaptogens and other plant-sourced alchemy for daily nourishment. || moonjuice.com

NATURAL SKINCARE

CAP Beauty || capbeauty.com

Living Libations This is a source for pure essential oils sourced only from plants. || livinglibations.com

PANTRY

Coconut Butter

CAP Beauty: The Coconut Butter || capbeauty.com/products/the-coconut-butter

Elemental Wizdom Here you can find wellness products with only the purest bioavailable ingredients available—no preservatives, artificial colors, flavors, sugars, gluten, yeast, soy, dairy, or casein. || elementalwizdom.com

Hot Sauce
Kauai Juice Co. || kauaijuiceco.com/collections/hot-sauce

Matcha
CAP Beauty: The Matcha || capbeauty.com/products/the-matcha

Miso
South River Miso || southrivermiso.com

Organic Coffee
Canyon Coffee || canyoncoffee.co

Plant Protein Powder
moonjuice.com/collections/plant-proteins || capbeauty.com

Probiotics
Klaire Labs || klaire.com

FERMENTED VEGETABLES

Hawthorne Valley || ferments.hawthornevalley.org

Thrive Market || thrivemarket.com

Ron Teeguarden's Dragon Herbs || dragonherbs.com

INDEX

263

265

267

269

ABOUT THE AUTHOR

Mafalda Pinto Leite is a world-traveling chef, mama, sustainable lifestyle leader, and passionate food educator. This mother of four has been researching, cooking, writing, and teaching about food, organic beauty, and health for the last twenty years.

Mafalda attended school for health-supportive culinary education at the Natural Gourmet Institute in NYC. In 2000, she graduated as a Certified Culinary Chef and Nutritional Practitioner. Then after fourteen years of nonstop evolution, she became a Certified Health Coach through the Institute for Culinary Nutrition and Herbalism.

After cooking school, she did her internship at The Millennium Restaurant, an award-winning gourmet vegan restaurant. She moved to Maui, where she worked at an exclusive yoga retreat and spa and then as a chef of Mana Foods, an iconic natural foods store in Paia. Next, in London, she worked at Jamie Oliver's first restaurant Monte's and at the bookshop Books for Cooks. She went back to New York in search of more in-depth knowledge of raw foods, where she worked for Matthew Kenney at the now shuttered Pure Food and Wine.

Mafalda now resides in Portugal, where she has six published books that have won awards like the Gourmand World Award and Best Health and Nutrition Book. In 2014, she created her own online shop, Puro Sumo, a resource for potent transformational foods for those seeking beauty, wellness, and longevity, to fulfill her own need to have access to the best affordable superfoods in the world through a simple click.

She now dedicates her creativity to her new online cooking school that offers sold-out workshops, empowering women to learn more about how to infuse intuition into cooking and to work with potent transformational plant-based beauty foods and high-powered natural remedies that nourish the mind, body, and spirit. You can learn more at www.mafaldapintoleite.com.